From Artichokes to Nairobi

Recipes, Travel, and Laughter

To my dear gun-slinging friend!
See page 86!

Love you!
Dianna Jackson

First edition   August 2023
Copyright © 2023   Dianna Jackson

Published by Penciled In
5319 Barrenda Ave
Atascadero, CA 93422
penciledin.com

ISBN-13:   978-1-939502-54-4

Book and Cover Design by Benjamin Daniel Lawless.

Text is set in Arno Pro and Canela Text.

From Artichokes to Nairobi

Recipes, Travel, and Laughter

DIANNA JACKSON

Author of the blog travelswiththerayman.com

Contents

A is for Artichokes 7
B is for Bananas 12
B is also for beans. I just couldn't help myself. 16
C is for Chocolate. What else? 21
D is for Dates 26
E is for Eggs & Egg Shells 29
F is for Finger Food 42
G is for Glorious Garlic 49
H is for Herbs 54
I is for Ice Cream 58
J is for Jalapeños 62
K is for Kitchen 64
L is for Love of Legs 68
M is for Macarons 73
N is for Nectarines 86
O is for Onions 91
P is for Poetic Pasta 95
Q is for Quail 98
R is for Rice 101
S is for Skeet 106
T is for Tomato 111
U is for Utensils 114
V is for Vinegar 118
W is for Watermelon 124
X is for Xmas Cookies 126
Y is for Yeasts 130
Z is for Zebra 133
Index of Recipes 142
Acknowledgements 144

Prologue

This book has been in the making since at **least** the engagement of George Clooney. That **is** quite a span of time. Luckily, what I have written is timeless!!

Picture taken at Stavalaura Vineyards and Winery in the state of Washington

> As you will discover, this book is about more than food.

Food doesn't happen in a vacuum. There are always **two** stories to tell about the food itself: the circumstances of the food and the importance of the food. Consider the birds of the world. They literally fly thousands of miles each year for their food. Nature shows are all about how animals stalk, kill, and eat their prey. It all boils down to food. And mating. But this book isn't about mating. It's all about food and the stories about that food.

So, dear reader, hope you grab a bite before you sit down to join me on this journey… a journey motivated by my love of food, travel, and writing. Without any of these, there would be nothing to read on the following pages.

Taken on the California coast at the Ragged Point Inn, Highway 1

Dedication

For Ryan and Tamara, I give you this book. And know that it would not have been possible but for the Rayman who appears throughout.

Love you.

Rayman

This artichoke was painted by Becky Dresser, a distant relative.

A is for Artichokes

Who would name a vegetable "artichoke"?

"If I eat it, will I choke?" comes to mind when you see or hear the word artichoke. The artichoke plant came from the Mediterranean region. It is not indigenous to the contiguous United States. And it's a thistle. OMG. A thistle that is perennial. The edible part of the plant is actually referred to as the bud. The bud is comprised of outer leaves which are technically referred to as bracts. The bracts have thorns at their tips. The bracts cover the heart. And when you pull a bract off, you scrape off a piece of the heart. Right above the heart is the choke which looks like hair, in a way. If left alone, the choke blooms and the artichoke bud looks like a flower. When looking for the derivation of the choke being the beard, I came across this website. "Does it make it harder to Choke a guy with a Beard?" Really. Impossible to make up.

But, I digress. Artichokes have benefitted from the care of the Europeans, the Arabs, and us. And since we live in California, I have to brag that California is responsible for 100% of the artichoke crops in the U.S. Furthermore, the Artichoke Capital of the World is located in Castroville. Castroville, and Watsonville which is right next door, produces 80% of the 100% of these artichoke crops according to Wikipedia. Having visited these two towns in Monterey county my whole life, I swear this information to be true. Miles and miles and miles and miles of artichoke fields. I think they are called fields. They wouldn't be referred to as orchards. That would sound funny. Ranches? No, that wouldn't be right. Farms? No, you need some livestock for farms. No, I do think it is fields.

Perhaps a creative advertising firm would brand this maligned thistle and name it "carciofo", its Italian name. Not sure how to pronounce it, but with enough repetition, people would adopt the name because it is so much more interesting. Carciofo hearts. Deep fried carciofo. Pickled carciofo. See what I mean?

Also, an artichoke is interesting to eat. What other vegetable is eaten by scraping then dissecting? This is a very tactile experience at once gratifying and, well, fun when it is served straight up and intact. It's like peeling back the layers of an onion without the onion. Each layer of the artichoke, oops, carciofo, reveals softer and sweeter "leaves" or bracts. Really, forget the bracts. I like the notion of scraping leaves between my teeth. Bracts just does not do it for me. Sometimes science is just too clinical for its own good. This is one of those times.

This is an artichoke plant up close and personal… in Portland, OR

Carciofos can be stuffed. There are all manners of cooking these wonderful thistles. Problem is there has never been an overwhelming amount of recipes for artichokes. That's because, I think, people east of the Rockies dominate the publishing world, and since they have to "import" the thistle, they don't eat it as much and, therefore, they don't write about it very much. But with the advent of the internet, it is a bit easier. And now you can watch YouTube for actual demos of dealing with carciofos. Pretty neat. But you may have to relent and google artichoke for more recipe choices. That is, until the advertising campaign moves into full swing.

So I guess at some point in the past — read the dawn of time — somebody noticed that the thistle was green. It grew. Therefore, it might be edible. And someone actually ate one. I imagine it was raw. And I am supposing that they scraped the leaves, and left the tough tops with those stickers because that instinctively seems like what our ancestors would have done. Then, how long do you suppose before someone came up with the notion of cooking it. My guess is that they probably barbecued it. And so I can understand why we are still eating them today. Barbecued artichokes are fabulous.

However, in my day and this age, I prefer to pre-cook them, marinate them, then saw them in half before throwing them on the barbie. When I was a kid, I loved (well, still do) steamed artichokes. Artichokes cooked to death in water were even good to me. Of course, my husband attributes this to my really loving the mayo. It is true…I like to dip them in mayo before scraping. However, there are other dips you could use, like butter to gild the bud, if I may. And you can dress up butter and mayo with things like garlic, anchovies, chutneys, flavored olive oil, plain EV (extra virgin) OO (olive oil) aka EVOO. (Readers aid: I'll use this acronym again perhaps so try to commit it to memory).

A cut up artichoke

Artichokes (I'm starting to change my mind. Maybe keeping the name artichoke will work if Madison Avenue comes up with a catchy phrase that portrays the artichoke as hip, cool) make certain food taste better. Steak and artichoke is a great combo. In the spirit of full disclosure, I don't eat beef much any more. Ever since I read the book *Omnivore's Dilemma*, I've cut back on meat. Michael Pollan wrote *Omnivore's Dilemma*, and it is a must-read after after you finish this book. But, if you do eat beef, you owe it to yourself to pair it with an artichoke. Perhaps Madison Avenue could have an eating demonstration on their ad to show people how to eat it. Quite possibly people steer clear of it because they don't see how it will work with a knife and fork. They could have a catchy tune playing and do it with a cartoon, even.

I can see it now. Some voice in the background intones, "Artichokes...hip, cool. And it is hip to be cool." Then they could have a disclaimer that people could read, "Not recommended for all eaters. Must be hip, cool. Must be able to eat with your fingers. So, cast away those silly old rules about not touching your food. Buy and eat an artichoke today." Or maybe they could use sex to sell the artichoke. Open with a sexy woman and man scraping their respective leaves and moaning as they do so. Then a voice-over saying, "buy one and eat it today. And see what happens." Oh, I could go on and on. But you get the idea. Here. The lines below are for you. Think up your own ad for the artichoke and write it down. It's fun. Do it. Today. See how you like it!!

Fun historical fact. Seems that the first Artichoke Queen of Castroville, CA was (drum roll, please), Marilyn Monroe. She was traveling around the area giving talks when the head of the Artichoke Organization for Castroville thought it would be a great idea for Marilyn and the 'choke to partner up. No Madison Avenue there. And she accepted. Now that is some trivia!!

There is another good thing about the artichoke. It's only 60 calories (eaten plain). And it is nutritious. So many virtues for this thistle. It is amazing.

So here's a recipe. In prose fashion.

1. Trim the artichoke, which means cut off the top of the leaves thereby getting rid of the thorns.

2. Throw some salt and pepper on the globe before steaming it. It generally takes about 1/2 hour. Or put it in a pressure cooker or Instant Pot and follow the manufacturer's instructions. After it is cooked (test by pulling out a leaf…it should yield easily), set it aside to cool. Once cooled, cut the artichoke down the middle and scrape or cut the choke out and discard.

3. Put the artichoke(s) in a non-corrosive container of your choice with some olive oil, a squeeze of fresh lemon, minced garlic, and herbs if you'd like. Cover and put in the refrigerator for a few hours or overnight.

4. Remove from the fridge. Bring it to room temperature if you have the time. Throw it on the grill (hopefully a wood burning grill) with the leaves on the bottom of the rack, and then sprinkle the top with your favorite cheese until the artichoke is warm and has picked up some color, and the cheese has melted slightly so that it looks barbecued.

Serve with your favorite dip. Voila. Fabulous. Easy. Delicious. Enjoy.
Pair with 2020 Dresser Winery Tempranillo.

 is for Bananas

It wasn't until I met and got to know an old friend, that I realized there were people who didn't like bananas. Really? There are people who don't love bananas? Right. They actually dislike bananas. This came as a complete shock to me. What's not to like?

Bananas are a perfect food. They are a dose of potassium (which I understand to be a very important mineral) wrapped up neatly in their own skin. If I were, say, a food designer judge, I would judge the banana to be an ideal food. It is a very sunny color (most of them are). They let you know how ripe they are without you having to "open it up" to find out. You can store them at room temperature. You can store them in the freezer in their protective wrapper. You can purposefully let them ripen completely (read get dark) so that they might be included in a recipe like banana nut bread. Or banana cake with chocolate swirls.

Bananas form on trees. This is a plus. Trees pull in carbon dioxide and water and use the energy of the sun to convert this into chemical compounds such as sugars to feed the tree. A by-product of that chemical reaction, oxygen, is produced and released by the tree. We need that oxygen for all life on earth. And, they grow in bunches (clumps) thereby making harvesting much easier. Now, there is a downside to bunches. In fairness of full disclosure, I must relay this story.

When I was about 8 years old, my Mom went to the store and bought a partial bunch of bananas. We were a banana-eating family. She deposited them on the counter in the kitchen. As a ravenous young tom-boy, I wanted something to eat, and before I knew it, all hell broke loose in the kitchen. Seems a big black spider came sauntering out of the partial bunch of bananas. Spiders do have the amazing ability to make themselves very small by folding themselves up with those limber legs of theirs. But I digress. This spider was of some tropical variety from parts unknown, and it was the biggest spider I had ever seen. And, I had seen some big spiders because tarantulas lived in our neck of the woods. It might have been a tarantula... when you are running around the kitchen looking for something with which to kill a spider, you really don't spend the time to categorize the spider. Anyway, that was hundreds of years ago; so I'm left with more of an impression than fact. But, I can report that the spider was huge. Ever since then, I have made it a habit to closely inspect, and sometimes shake the partial bunch of bananas before snapping off one to eat.

Maybe a spider sprang forth and alarmed my friend. Perhaps he was scared by a spider, and that is why he doesn't like bananas. Because you can't really kill a spider with a gun, and this guy was a gun guy. He loved guns. He was a card-carrying member of the NRA... he wanted the right to kill a spider with a gun if he needed to. Really, I think killing a spider with a gun is not a good idea. It would be too messy. It would cause too much damage. Innocent by-standers might be hurt. "Really, officer, I didn't mean to shoot my wife. I was aiming at the spider. She walked into the kitchen to get a banana when I squeezed the trigger, and the bullet boomeranged off the counter and hit her."

See what I mean?

As I have grown older, there are many interesting things that have happened involving the banana. I have learned that bananas, when left in one's golf bag, get ripe in about 12 holes, on average. If you forget that you have a banana in your golf bag until the end of the round, it will only be suitable for dumping in the garbage unless you like really, really mushy bananas; or you plan to bake banana nut bread. This is assuming that the banana started out ripe, read yellow, not green.

There is also an art to eating a banana. Doesn't it just drive you to drink when you try to peel a banana, and you can't get the pliable skin to break open? You twist it. You bend it. It just doesn't want to open. Well, you could learn a thing or two about bananas from apes and chimpanzees. They never have a problem. Admittedly, they have eaten a lot more bananas in their day than I have. I think that is true. I know it is true that they have eaten more bananas than my old friend. Anyway, watch a monkey or ape eat a banana. They do not open it from the end that was attached to the bunch. They open it from the other end. The end end if you will.

And it works like a charm.

You see. We can learn from others. Our not-too-distant relatives, the primates, know what they are doing when it comes to bananas. Check it out the next time you go to the zoo. Or fly to Africa. Which reminds me.

Around 1988 I flew to Africa with my Uncle Ralph. We were in Tanzania out on the great Serengeti. There were plenty of monkeys and baboons there. And, in this case, it was the baboons about which we were warned. It seems that in the lodges located within the Serengeti, word had spread within the baboon community that there was food to be had in the guest rooms. Many tourists bring hard candies to give to the African children they meet on their travels. Some tourists may bring candies for themselves to eat as well. So, we were warned about this by our guide. He told us to lock our doors. Secure our rooms.

Here is the thing about groups. There is always someone who does not follow instructions. There is, invariably, someone who is also a pain in the derriere (a French term), and it is not necessarily the same person. Anyway. Our group was no different. It included a couple who forgot to lock their door and window before going out for a game ride. When they returned to their room after the ride, it looked like the police had raided their room looking for drugs. Suitcases were opened. Clothes were thrown here and there. Toiletries had been opened. The baboons had descended on their room and searched for food. No bananas present, they found the candy. And the tourists lost a few things in the exchange.

This story does nothing to illustrate how to peel a banana. But believe me when I tell you... if the baboons had found a banana, they would have peeled it from the end end.

Once, I decided to try making a banana cream pie. I had clipped an article out of the L.A. Times and filed it in my food binder where it remained for years. Finally, I discovered that Larry, my cousin Susie's husband, loved banana cream pie. They were coming to visit so I had the perfect occasion to make that pie. The only problem was that there was no crust recipe. It just specified a graham cracker crust. Well. I jumped on-line and looked for a recipe. Emeril of "bam" fame had a recipe listed, and I figured he knew what he was talking about. Somehow I had it in my mind that you could get a good banana cream pie in New Orleans. And, if you could, Emeril would know how to make that crust. So, that is how I ended up with the recipe.

I made the crust and then I made the pie. Well. Things didn't go so well as evidenced by the fact that we really needed a jack hammer to cut through the crust, and we needed a spoon to eat the runny custard pie filling. OMG. The crust was inedible. The recipe called for it to be baked for 10 minutes. Really. I didn't know this was a bad idea because Mr. Bam had instructed me to do so. But what that 10 minutes did was to turn the crust into something quite suitable for, say, a dental filling...it was hard as a rock and may have lasted for years if I hadn't chucked it into the garbage. Didn't put it down the garbage disposal. It would have probably broken it, or, at the very least, the racket could have caused severe ear damage.

And the soup of a filling. Quite tasty, but it made for a horrible presentation. To this day my cousin taunts me with memories of that banana cream pie by saying things like, "Oh, yes. I certainly remember that banana cream pie. Please don't make that again." She really knows how to hurt a person even though she kids me.

My plan is to make another banana cream pie, but I can report definitively that I will not use the recipes I thought would be so good.

From one of my favorite magazines comes this recipe. Put it in your browser and take a gander.

My other banana recipe that I love is made thus.

1. Peel the banana.
2. Split it in half length-wise.
3. Spread your favorite peanut butter on it.
4. Stick it back together.
5. Then enjoy your banana & peanut butter sandwich. Yum.

B is also for beans. I just couldn't help myself.

They are so nutritious, inexpensive, and easy that a word or two must be written about beans.

*"Beans, beans, the musical fruit
The more you eat, the more you toot."*

There is much truth to the old rhyme. Beans are a fruit. Who knew? I have known that rhyme my whole life and I guess I never really thought about it. But, beans are fruits. Perhaps you can now use this information in a game of Trivial Pursuit.

Everyone should know how to cook a pot of beans. It is just a requirement. It is so easy, but it takes planning ahead. Beans are best if soaked overnight in a big bowl of water. It rehydrates them a bit. Cooking them doesn't take as long if they are soaked.

I drain the soaking water and put new water (or other liquids) in the pot. One red onion cut into quarters is a nice addition. I fill my pot to about 3 inches above the beans, bring them to a boil and then turn the heat down to low so they can simmer until tender. If the lily must be gilded, a ham hock is also a good addition to the bean pot. If no meat is added, salt your beans toward the end. Or not. I think beans benefit from salt. But the bean community rages over the controversy of when to salt. I'm thinking it is just not that critical. Salt when you want. The main event is that you are cooking beans at home and for a fraction of the cost of canned beans.

Beans freeze after they have been cooked. So, if you don't need a whole pound of beans, cook them anyway and then freeze for another meal at another time. Simple and elegant, those beans.

Beans and tomato sauce

DIRECTIONS:

1 Pick over beans and discard any that look out of place. Or small pebbles.

2 Cover the beans with 3-inches of water and allow beans to soak overnight.

3 Drain the beans, place them in the pot along with cut onion and ham hock, then cover with 3-inches of water. Bring to a boil and boil for about 10 minutes.

4 Reduce heat and simmer for 1 hour. Test for doneness. Beans should be soft. If not, simmer until they are soft. Add salt the last 30 minutes of cooking.

INGREDIENTS:

- Dried beans such as pink beans - 1/2 lb to 1 lb.
- Water
- Onion, cut into quarters
- Ham hock if desired
- Salt

Pair with 2020 Dresser Winery Zinfandel

NOTA BENE:

You can also go on line and find thousands of recipes so I'm not going to reinvent the internet here. The main thing, and I can't say this enough, is to cook your own beans and you'll be glad you did. It only takes one pot for the beans, one knife for the onion. Really. Amen.

However, if you don't have time, you can resort to the Instant Pot to cook your beans according to manufacturer's directions. Or, you can buy canned beans. Sometimes we just don't have time, do we?

Canned beans are cooked perfectly. So, use them if you must. Canners of beans do a good job. You will be fine.

For years, we traveled around in an RV. RVs are great for eliminating the need to eat out while on the road. On the other hand, RV cooking can be difficult and with RV cooks everywhere, I include this story for your pleasure … or warning! The story below was written and posted on my blog on June 24, 2014.

Cooking on the head of a pin. That's what cooking in an RV is like. And that's what I've been doing this a.m. while Rayman is away at Tahoe Donner playing one of the prettiest golf courses known to man (in this neck of the woods). Coyote Moon. Don't you just love that name for a golf course? Think of the logo possibilities, for heaven's sake. A coyote howling at the moon, anyone? Coyote jumping over the moon? Maybe not. Dancing around a moon? That might work.

But I digress. The blog below was written on June 24, 2014.

" Today I'm making black bean chili and this requires a shout-out to Margaret Fox who owned the restaurant in Mendocino, Cafe Beaujolais. I bought her cookbook years ago. It has been reduced to frayed pages, juice-spotted pages, a paperback without a spine, essentially. They just don't bind books the way they used to. This cookbook has been falling apart for years. I am guessing it is about 40 years old. Maybe 30. Who's counting?

There I go again. This recipe is fabulous. There is no meat in it. None. Zip. Yet, it tastes like it does in a way. That's because of the black beans. I bought organic black beans from a food co-op in a town up the road. The town, Portola s inhabited by 2,500 people, and they have a co-op which I find amazing. However, there must not be many Mexicans around because these beans have been cooking for quite a long time and they aren't completely soft … and, yes, I soaked them all night. I would guess they have been in the bin since the last millennium. But, be that as it may, the dish is worth waiting for. Served with shredded cheese, fresh green onions, cilantro and sour cream … yummy.

You are probably wondering if I have that cookbook with me. Well, no I don't. But I do have the computer and googled the recipe, and now it is time to give a shout-out to Russ Parsons of the L.A. Times food section for publishing the recipe in the newspaper. So, there you have it.

Now about this head of the pin stuff. In order to chop, chop, chop the onions, the garlic, the bell pepper, the jalapeños, one must use a cutting board and in order to use a cutting board, one must make space in the kitchen to lay the thing down. This requires that I cover up half my sink to make room. I must be neat and tidy or the place will end up looking like Camp Poody. Ah, another skill set being developed here. At home I just fling things around with free abandon as I have oodles of space.

The other thing is this. There is limited storage space so I have already run out of Hungarian paprika (the red can), cumin seeds, cayenne and olive oil (not EVOO). Oh, and I'm dangerously low on peppercorns. Good thing Rayman is in Truckee. I've already sent him a list of necessities including rum for mojitos. Found a "muddler" at a local little gift store and made it a gift to myself so I'm dying to try it. Yikes. I need to add mint to the list of groceries. Also, the refrigerator is quite small. While at Costco, I espied a bag of limes and it was such a good buy (read going broke saving money) that I bought it and it takes up approximately half the refrigerator. Perhaps a slight exaggeration. But it does take up one whole drawer. Mojitos anyone? Come on by and I'll fix you up!!

"Hi dearie, Along with all the other groceries I need, add fresh mint to the list. For the mojitos, a good cause if there ever was one. Hope you are making some birdies". (kiss up, kiss up). That's how I'll compose my email to him without the kiss up part.

I just hope I don't run out of propane before these darn beans are cooked. That's the other thing about RVs. You have what I refer to as a "heightened awareness" of all things utilitarian like propane, water, gray sewage etc. Never give that stuff a second thought at home unless PG&E turns off the juice. If that happens it is a great excuse to go out to dinner. Here, I am stuck. No car. And I certainly don't want to drive to a restaurant in the RV. That would require messing around with the sewer hookup. Nah. Not doing that!! Anyway, it might look a bit weird to pull up to a restaurant in a 33-foot behemoth for a plate of spaghetti. Just saying. I am, however, very glad I know how to drive the thing. If I needed to go somewhere, I could.

I'm giving the beans 5 more minutes. They are finally getting soft.

Well, I waited for 5 minutes and they still are *al dente*. Drats.

So, while I am composing this blog, I am hearing a bit of racket outside. I looked out the door and this is what I saw. This park needs more trash bins. Last night when I went to dump my garbage can (did I mention that our garage can is about 5 gallons?), I couldn't get the dumpster can open. Turns out they lock them up because of bears. So, while I was struggling with trying to get one of the cans open, a man and woman sauntered by with an empty pizza box (I guess empty based on their sizes). I enlisted their help. They were forthcoming. The bins were completely full. Now, this morning they are bulging and hence, the owner of the park, is now jumping up and down on them.

Look closely at the picture of the man on the trash can in the next photo.

The beans needed more water. Need I say more?

The thing is, this park is full of RVs and short on people. Many sites have RVs hooked up and locked up. No one is home. The people to our right haven't been here since we arrived. The people on our left, left. That was after we introduced ourselves and discovered in about 1 minute of the conversation that they had spent the afternoon "in that brewery up at the end of a dirt road nearby". Then she proceeded to praise Cliven Bundy, the crazy rancher near Mesquite, NV because "enough is enough". And he pointed to his beer, a Negra Modela, and said he was drinking the Negra in honor of our President, wink wink. I said, "Ouch." Then as she went on about Cliven's point of view and how she thought he was right, I interjected, "Well. Here's the thing. I love Obama. So let's just agree to disagree. We don't need to talk politics." And he said, "Or religion." And while having a discussion sans politics, we discover that he is a retired truck driver and didn't have to pay for health care because he got it through his union (but his union was not like those rotten unions back east) and she hated Obamacare and she retired from a school district (lordy, I hope she wasn't a teacher). And that was that. Except, did I mention that he sat there all afternoon outside the RV drinking beer and smoking cigars and playing his playlist on their outdoor speakers? So, after dinner while the Rayman and I were engrossed in a challenging game of Scrabble while listening to Roy Orbison croon from the speaker next door (actually his playlist wasn't bad), we kept hearing him tell her to "shut up and sit down" and "we'll discuss it in the morning" and "you are drinking too much, sit down", and "don't drink so much", and "I'm not picking you up off the floor again." OMG. So, the next morning, the poor guy slinked out of the RV park with his wife and we haven't seen them since. He knew we had to move spots on Thursday and my money was on them not returning until the next people moved in. Just saying.

So, the beans are done, we still have propane, and I'm going to sign off for now. It's time to read my book about Lewis and Clark. Want to get it done before we hit Oregon on July 20.

Good day."

C is for Chocolate. What else?

Chocolate. Need I say more?

Chocolate is one of the finest things on earth. It is right up there with Yosemite. Chocolate is to food as Yosemite is to scenery. Doesn't get much better than that. And, if you haven't been to Yosemite, you must go. Drop everything, jump on that plane and/or jump in that car and head down or up the road. You will not regret it.

This is one shot of Yosemite looking up.

I digress, people.

Chocolate should only be eaten alone or with someone. It should be dark, the chocolate, that is. Dark chocolate is much healthier than other chocolate. Milk chocolate has, well, milk. No. Chocolate should be dark and at least 60% cocoa. My opinion, but I have had years of practice and my early years were wasted. Wasted on milk chocolate. I just didn't know. Now, in this day and age when you can google anything, you can find out for yourself. Or ask your doctor. As long as your doc isn't a crank.

Julia Child was an amazing woman. I'm sure she went to Yosemite many times. She probably ate at the Ahwahnee Hotel. Oh, the Ahwahnee. Noted for it's infuriatingly small parking lot. But, maybe they have a point. The Ahwahnee Hotel is a man-made must-see in the park, and that is why the parking lot is impossible. Because almost everyone who enters the park brings their car. Or their motorcycle. Wouldn't it be wonderful if they restricted cars? Handicapped people should be allowed to drive in. Everyone else should board a bus to get in the park. It is too small for the number of cars. The air gets spoiled with car fumes. The air becomes hazy. Did I mention the parking? It is horrid. Worse than a Trader Joe's parking lot. The time is now. Ban autos and motorcycles (unless they have mufflers.) I can only imagine what the park would be like with no noise other than leaves rustling, water flowing and falling. I'm not religious, but it would be akin to a religious experience for those who are religious. And for people like me, it would just be awesome. And quiet.

Perhaps my Grandmother is responsible for all this that I am. She was a good cook. An engaged cook and she took time to encourage me just like I'm taking time to encourage you!! So a few years ago, I belonged to the Assistance League, a philanthropic group that helped clothe disadvantaged children. To raise money, the group decided to publish a cookbook. Well, that was right up my alley. However, they wanted recipes from members that were "authentic". Passed down from another generation perhaps. So, after thinking about this, I came up with two recipes. One was for pink beans. The other was for Black Bottom Pie.

Now, my Grandmother's name (real name) was Birdie. I wanted to give her her due in this cookbook. So I submitted the black bottom pie recipe, and it was accepted. When the cookbook came out, we were asked to check it to make certain it passed muster. OMG. The recipe was entitled, "Birdie Dresser's Black Bottom." Somehow the word pie was missing. OMG. I flew into sheer panic because, you see, we live in a small county (250,000 people) and my grandmother was an attendant to the Pioneer Day parade's queen one year. She was known. She served on the Library Board of Paso Robles. Families knew her. Yes, she had by this time passed on, but I was horrified! This situation could not stand. After much consideration, I had the publisher, at my expense, reprint the page and mail me replacements for all 500 or so books which I then painstakingly went through to pull and replace the offending page. The book was a three-ringed binder affair. It took forever. And it cost a fortune. But in the end, pardon the pun, the recipe was changed to Black Bottom Pie ala Birdie Dresser. Here's the recipe. It is really good and light. And, horrors upon horrors, it doesn't use dark chocolate. But for the sake of the story...

Black Bottom Pie

DIRECTIONS:

Mix gelatin, sugar and salt in top of double boiler. Combine egg yolk and milk and mix with gelatin mixture. Chop 3 oz. chocolate and add to mixture. Cook over boiling water until chocolate is melted. Remove from heat and whisk until smooth. Chill until thickened. Add the vanilla to the icy cold evaporated milk and whip it until frothy. Fold the chilled chocolate mixture into the evaporated milk. Pile into baked pie shell and chill. Before serving, spread top with whipped cream except for about a three-inch circle in the center so the chocolate filling remains exposed. Shave remaining ounce of chocolate into long curls with a vegetable peeler. Place on whipped cream with widest curls upright. Serves 6-8.

INGREDIENTS:

- 1 envelope gelatin
- 3/4 c. sugar
- 1/8 tsp. salt
- 1 egg yolk, slightly beaten
- 3/4 c. whole milk
- 4 oz. unsweetened chocolate
- 1 c. icy cold evaporated milk
- 1 tsp. vanilla
- 1 9-in. baked pie shell
- 1 c. whipped cream, whipped and sweetened. (Avoid the pre-whipped cream that comes in a can.)

No Mousse au Chocolat, but a very good pie. Do not use graham cracker crust. Use a real crust—made with flour, butter, water, and salt.

Now, where was I with this dark chocolate thing? I have to interrupt myself to announce that my friend, Margaret, just called me and was bereft. George Clooney is engaged. (That is an indication of how long I've been working on this book.) This is almost as bad as a chocolate shortage. George Clooney. Engaged. Margaret and I will not alter our plans to stalk him at some future date. He is too beautiful to be left alone. Or should I have said, delicious?

So. Dark chocolate. Yum. One of my favorite desserts is dark chocolate and Syrah wine. Or dark chocolate and Zin. Or dark chocolate and Cab. A square or two washed down with red wine is heaven sent. We buy good French dark chocolate. No Hershey's here. No sirree. A cut above for this kid. With good red wine. No Ripple. No Charles Shaw (Two Buck Chuck). Good wine like Dresser or Opolo. Or Le Cuvier. Or Linne. Paso Robles red. It is dark and chewy. Love the stuff. Or Port. Love it with Port.

If you want to eat the most fabulous chocolate mousse, head right to the cookbook Julia Child wrote and cook away. There is not a better recipe out there. It has no whipped cream. The dish is comprised of butter, eggs, chocolate, coffee, liqueur. And sugar. Time consuming? Yes. Difficult? A bit. But her instructions are perfect and so, if you can read, you can make this dessert. And it makes a lot of rich, scrumptious mousse. Enough for 12, I'm thinking. See E is for Eggs for the full recipe and instructions if you don't "own" Julia.

Something else that is the rage is the molten lava cake. It is a lovely dessert too.

Molten Chocolate Cake

SAUCE:

- 4 1/2 ounces bittersweet or semi-sweet chocolate chopped
- 2 ounces unsweetened chocolate chopped
- 1/3 c. hot water
- 1/4 c. light corn syrup
- 3/4 tsp. peppermint extract

CAKE:

- 5 ounces bittersweet chocolate chopped
- 10 Tbsp. unsalted butter
- 3 large eggs
- 3 large egg yolks
- 1 1/2 c. powdered sugar
- 1/2 c. all purpose flour
- Ice cream

1. Chop chocolate. Place in top of a double boiler and melt over simmering water. Be careful not to overcook chocolate. Add hot water, corn syrup and extract and whisk until smooth. You can do this ahead of time and re-warm before serving.

2. For the cake, chop the chocolate. Melt the chocolate and butter together over simmering water in the top of a double boiler. Separate egg yolks from 3 three eggs and add them to the three eggs in a bowl. Beat them for several minutes. This will prevent them from cooking when you add the chocolate mixture. Add the powdered sugar and beat to incorporate. Combine the chocolate and butter slowly into the eggs and sugar until just incorporated. Do the same with the flour using a spatula. Don't over mix as it will deflate the eggs.

3. Pour into six ramekins. This can be done ahead of time. Cover and refrigerate if not using immediately.

4. Heat oven to 400. Place in the middle of oven and cook 11 minutes or 14 minutes if refrigerated. They are done when they appear shiny on top and start to firm up. Do not overcook. Remove from oven and run knife around each cake before turning on to a plate. Once out, flip it so that it is right side up and serve with a scoop of ice cream.

What is so appealing about this recipe is that it can be made ahead of time and placed in the refrigerator until you are ready to cook it. Great for entertaining. The sauce is optional. It is good either way.

 is for Dates

Not all snacks are created equal. And dates prove it. I consider them a perfect food on many levels. And I am often surprised when people state that they don't like dates. Taste buds differ. I get that. But dates?

Now that California is in a huge drought, dates may become more popular. That's because they need just about no water to survive and produce dates. Dates hate humidity so that is why all those date trees you see in L.A. or Santa Barbara never bear fruit. The dates will not ripen in moist air. Date growers who live in the Coachella Valley of California are not worried about the lack of water, perhaps. Virtually all the dates grown there are consumed in the U.S. Which is interesting since California is not on the list of major date producers. Far and away, the Middle East and north Africa produce the most dates. Hot and dry. The dates need hot and dry. In fact, one of those big date producing countries hasn't seen a drop of rain in over two years. Now…that is dry. Which may explain why date trees manage to stand tall against the wind. They must have deep roots. Don't know. Just thinking that might be the case. Roots digging down deep to tap underground moisture.

Dates are very popular in the Middle East. They are mentioned in the Bible as well as the Koran. Many times. So, they have been around a long time. People like them because they are sweet and don't spoil. You can take them on a caravan into the Sahara or, just as easily, take them in your golf bag for a quick boost of energy on the golf course. I consider them a perfect fruit. They have lots of potassium and iron and there are articles that suggest that they make giving birth easier. And who is against that, for heavens sakes?

But I digress.

We always keep dates on hand. They are terrific for quick snacks and quick appetizers. Bacon wrapped dates that are stuffed with goat cheese and an almond are a real crowd pleaser. Throw some cut up dates in a salad to exploit the ying-yang of life. One of my very favorite cookie recipes at holiday time includes an anise/date/fig paste, spread over a cookie dough and rolled into a log and cut before baking into disks. Truly wonderful stuff. See the X-mas cookie chapter.

My grandmother added chopped dates to her fruit cocktail at Thanksgiving. In November, oranges were in season so there were always oranges, apples, walnuts, dates and a maraschino cherry to crown the concoction. Not sure she dressed the salad. She just used the fruit juice. A satisfying fruit salad dressing can be made with mayo and honey. Mix and drizzle as you wish.

Easy. Delicious.

The dates were always my favorite part of that fruit cocktail. So throw away that canned fruit cocktail. Opt for fresh and natural.

If you use apples, douse them in fresh lemon juice to keep them from turning brown. There are also flavored oils like walnut oil, almond oil, tangerine olive oil, avocado oil that could be used to dress the salad. And some chopped mint would provide a splash of taste and color.

Incidentally, this is the website for the avocado store we love (Morro Creek Ranch). If you are in our neck of the woods, I highly recommend a stop at their stand.

Bacon Wrapped Dates

with Goat Cheese or Blue Cheese and a Nut of your choice

INGREDIENTS:

- 18 pitted dates
- About 2 ounces of goat cheese
- 18 almonds
- 6 slices of bacon

Pair with 2021 Dresser Winery Kaia Lee

DIRECTIONS:

1. Let the goat cheese come to room temperature. Cut the slices of bacon into thirds, crossway.

2. Slice the dates open with kitchen scissors by cutting through the hole left from pitting the dates. (Most dates have a small hole through the center).

3. Open up the date and use a pastry bag or a skinny spoon to pipe goat cheese into the center of the date. Add an almond and close the date. Wrap a piece of bacon around the date. Continue assembling the dates and place them on a parchment-lined baking sheet with the seam of the bacon facing down.

4. Bake at 350 degrees for 15 - 20 minutes, until the bacon is crispy. Place the bacon-wrapped dates on a paper towel to absorb any extra grease; then serve. You can assemble the bacon-wrapped dates a day ahead and rewarm.

E is for Eggs & Egg Shells

So, which came first, the chicken or the egg? A fabulous question to contemplate, and really, that cause-and-effect question still looms large, doesn't it? In all walks of life. The universe begs the question. It beguiles me, and it probably beguiles you, too. Because the chicken/egg question is so, well, embedded in our pysche, the author must take on both the chicken and the egg in this chapter. For without one, you will not have the other.

Eggs are a many-splendored thing. Again the packaging. It is marvelous. The eggshell is so durable, it will clog your pipes. To be specific, it will clog your drain pipes if you throw the shells down the garbage disposal. This knowledge comes directly from the experience of my husband, Rayman. Rayman joined a group called Indian Guides which was organized through the YMCA (yes, you may jump up and go thru the motions while singing along). Its mission was to get fathers and sons together in an organized setting with other fathers and sons so that everyone could bond. Cumbaya. Cumbaya. And it worked!! The fathers named their tribe, the Choctaws. And they still call themselves the Choctaws. To my way of thinking, they are a wild and crazy bunch of guys. The boys, oops, sons? Oh, they grew up, grew apart and moved on. Not the dads. They haven't grown up, and they haven't moved on. They still get together regularly. One of the get-togethers used to take place at our house once a year. A weekend of wine, poker and golf. A great time was had by all. I ran away and stayed someplace else. No women allowed. That was the rule.

These guys are well-established men in their professions. Officers of companies, lawyers, engineers, architects, stockbrokers, insurance guy turned pecan farmer. Their wit is only exceeded by their net worth. Actually, that is not true. They are all very, very funny. I love these guys. We have on occasion had mixed parties and that is when we women get to witness the wits on display. It is a sight to behold.

But I digress.

So, as mentioned previously, they used to come to our house once a year for a party that generally lasted three days, two nights. And, during that time, they would play two rounds of golf, two nights of poker... and they cooked. When it first started out, I made the food and attached stick-ems with instructions on the dishes in the fridge. Now, they do all the shopping, all the cooking, all the clean-up. Much easier on me. But that is not the point. The point is they COOKED. And usually, they fixed a big breakfast with eggs and all the things that go along with eggs in the morning. So, there were 6 guys and they each ate at least 2 eggs and all those eggshells were deposited into the garbage disposal which ground them up and swallowed them. For awhile.

At 2:00 a.m after poker was done, Rayman headed down to bed and found in the master bath, a mess of gigantic proportions. The eggshells had clogged the drain. Dirty water was in the sinks, in the drawers, on the floor. It took him hours to clean it all up. And that's how I know that eggshells clog drains.

Nevertheless, that being said, eggshells are pretty nifty. And what's inside is better still. Eggs aren't just loved by people...all sorts of animals love eggs. Foxes, coyotes, birds. They all eat eggs. Snakes eat eggs. Bad visual there. But you get the drift. Eggs are a good source of nutrition, ready for the breaking.

As a cook, I have had much experience working with eggs. I love meringue (a French word). It is easy to make, and it is used in many a recipe. Every cook should know how to make meringue. It is like learning how to boil water or cook a steak. Elemental, I say. Having said that, I did have problems with whipping some egg whites yesterday. You cannot get anything in egg whites (read yolk), or they will not expand. It's just chemistry, but it is true. And when I broke open the egg, the yolk broke. I thought I managed to capture the white without any yolk but after several minutes of beating on high, the whites would not gain volume. What a bummer because I was out of eggs. This meant Rayman had to go to the store and buy a dozen eggs. And then I had to start all over. The dessert I was making (a frozen praline/banana parfait) was estimated to take 45 minutes to make. Scratch that. Who does that estimating anyway? It always takes longer than the estimated time. My time just kept getting longer because the recipe called for hazelnuts. Well, I had a bag of hazelnuts but it seemed to me that they were quite old. Uhm. No expiration date noted. So, I put the required amount of nuts in boiling water with some baking soda and cooked them for 4 minutes. This is how to remove hazelnut skins easily...it's easy but time consuming. I'm sure that was not factored in to this recipe. Then, after I misread the recipe and prepared twice as many nuts as were required...I discovered to my dismay that the nuts tasted rancid. EEEEEEEKKKKKKKK. What to do?

Well, Seabrook, one of the Indian Guide dads, had moved to Oklahoma to become a pecan farmer; and he sent us some spicy pecans from his pecan orchard. I stored the nuts in my freezer. Actually most of my nuts are stored in the freezer...they last much longer. But I digress.

So, Seabrook, yes...that's his name...his first name, sent these pecans and since they were spicy, I decided to substitute them in the dessert for the hazelnut pralines, thereby avoiding making the pralines which involved melting sugar in water and making caramel. What a great idea. So that's what I did, and that ended up saving me about 1/2 hour of further work. My 45 minutes had already taken about an hour of work...and I wasn't done yet.

Oh, and yes, I did throw the hazelnuts away... all of them.

So, when you make meringue and break a yolk... throw the egg away. It will not work. Ever.

On the next page is my adapted version of the Gordon Ramsay recipe I used.

Frozen Praline & Banana Parfait

DIRECTIONS:

To prepare, get a small loaf pan (6" x 3") and cut parchment paper to fit it lengthwise and enough left on either side to cover it once filled.

Okay. You crush the pralines by putting them in the food processor to grind or put them in a baggie and hit the heck out of them with a blunt, heavy object. Set aside.

Peel the 2 bananas (these are better ripe with some brown on the skin) and smash them up and add 1 tsp. of lemon juice to them. Add the crushed pralines (except for 4 tbsp) into the bananas. Set aside.

Then whip the cream. The cream should not be whipped stiff. Semi stiff, please. Like starting to make peaks...but not quite. You don't want it runny.

Then, in a separate bowl, whip the egg whites and gradually add the sugar as you whip them to stiff, shiny peaks.
Gently fold the whipped cream into the egg whites. Add the bananas and pralines and gently fold in.

Pour this batter into the parchment paper-lined loaf pan, cover and freeze.

10 minutes before serving, take the parfait out of the freezer and place in the fridge. Then heat a dry pan, peel the remaining bananas, slice them length-wise into irregular pieces, sprinkle with sugar and throw them in the pan turning when the bananas turn brown from the caramelized sugar. While they cook, form a narrow line with the set-aside pralines in the middle of each serving plate. Put some banana on one side of the pralines on each plate and a slice of parfait on the other side of the praline line on the plate. And serve.

You will love it. So good. It will take longer than 45 minutes. But if you have everything on hand and you don't get yolk in your whites, it should only take an hour to an hour and fifteen minutes to complete.

NOTA BENE:

I don't hesitate to eat uncooked eggs, but this is not recommended. So, do what you think is right.

INGREDIENTS:

- 4 ounces spicy pecans or store bought pralines (or you can make your own) Put aside about 4 Tbsp. for garnish.
- 2 ripe bananas (the skin should be very spotty, but not bruised or black)
- 2 tsp. lemon juice
- 1 ⅓ c. whipping cream
- 2 egg whites
- ½ c. sugar
- 4 ripe, but firm bananas
- ½ c. sugar

Great do-ahead dessert.

Eggs are the star ingredient in many a dish. Quiches, mousses (or is it moussi?), macarons, pavlovas, frittatas, pastas. Even salads. And the French and Italians really perfected the use of eggs as evidenced by the names above. The Chinese came up with 100 year old eggs. And the list goes on. Really, would you ever eat a 100 year old egg? I personally cannot imagine doing that. And, quite frankly, I just lack the nerve.

But I will eat chocolate mousse. And, I think that Julia Child published the ultimate chocolate mousse recipe. Yummy. But don't try this at home unless you know how to work with eggs.

We have discussed meringue but not to any great length. There are a few more tricks about egg whites. Whip them when they are at room temp. When incorporating other ingredients into the whipped whites, make certain that you fold gently with a whisk held palm down to start and curling your palm toward you so that the palm ends up (*Dianna-this direction is as clear as mud!*). This note is from my Editor, Nancy Cleland. I love it and think it adds a bit of personality to this cookbook. So I left it in.

This maneuver equals one fold. Take as few folds as possible, because the more you play with the meringue, the more the egg whites will lose the air you have beaten into them. Those tricks are the most important.

With egg yolks, you have a whole different set of circumstances. Yolks thicken things. In order to make them thick, heat is used. However, if you put a yolk in a pan and put the pan on the heat, the yolk will cook. This will ruin any dish. So, you whip the egg yolks first. This will give you insurance against cooking the egg yolk. Again, it is chemistry. Always whip the yolk if you are applying heat in any way to the yolk. Cardinal rule.

Let's see. Where was I? Oh, yes. Julia Child. When I started getting really interested in cooking, I bought *Mastering the Art of French Cooking* and *Julia Child's Kitchen*. And, perhaps the first thing I did was make Julia Child's Mousse au Chocolat. And that is probably my first introduction to various chocolates, because I think she gave me a choice of chocolates to use. Of course, in those days the only chocolate offered was Baker's chocolate. And that's what I used. But it still came out great and was a revelation. Her Mousse au Chocolat was made simply of chocolate, coffee, eggs, Grand Marnier, and sugar. It is a labor intensive dessert, but so worth it. No whipped cream. All the volume comes from the way you treat those eggs. You temper (beat) the egg yolks, beat the egg whites. Melt the chocolate carefully. If you pay no attention to the chocolate, you will spoil the dessert. Chocolate needs to only melt. Over-melting will burn the chocolate and make it grainy. I'm sure Alton Brown can tell you why. I'm just saying that it is true. I've screwed up lots of chocolate in my life. A very sad situation which then requires the cook to throw out the chocolate and start anew. So, one must respect that chocolate for superior results. And, if you do, you will end up with a magnificent mousse. Dark, deep, almost mysterious in its difficult simplicity. That is, if you don't get water in your eggs.

This dish requires the cook to gently simmer a pan of water into which the bowl with the egg yolks are placed. Then beat the yolks with a hand-held mixer. A large double boiler might work. Anyway. What could go wrong? Eggs on the cabinets? Water in the eggs? Pans on the floor. Almost anything imaginable can happen. This is not a dish for the faint of heart. But that is another reason why it is so good. As Yogi Berra once said, "90% of the game is half mental," and that's the truth. Ninety percent of cooking is half mental. You read the recipe and say, "I can't do that" because it looks difficult. But that may be a mental game you are playing on yourself. Put your brain on ice and try it. You may be pleasantly surprised. And, if it doesn't work, you'll have a story, anyway.

So, Julia took some eggs, some chocolate, some strong coffee, some sugar, some Grand Manier, some butter and came up with a truly remarkable mousse.

Mousse au Chocolat

AN ASIDE:

There is a term in french cooking called "mise en place". It means, get all your stuff gathered and measured so you can just make the recipe without a lot of stopping and starting. A great way to cook which I highly recommend and don't always do. When I don't do it, I always regret it.

So, in that spirit, gather together the following:

- 3-qt. stainless steel bowl (for egg yolks)
- A clean, dry stainless steel bowl for beating egg whites. I use my KitchenAid standard mixer bowl.
- A small saucepan for the coffee mixture.
- A portable electric beater.
- A larger pan pan with 1 or 2 inches of simmering water, to hold the small pan. I use a small double boiler. This is used for melting the chocolate. Modern women might use the microwave, but this method can be quite tricky.
- Another even larger pan with simmering water into which to set the egg-yolk pan.
- A bowl of water with some ice cubes.
- 1 or 2 rubber spatulas (scrapers)

INGREDIENTS:

- 4 large eggs
- 1-1/2 tsp. instant coffee dissolved in 1/4 c. hot water
- 3/4 c. sugar
- 1/4 c. orange liquor (Grand Marnier or Cointreau)
- 4-1/2 oz. semi-sweet baking chocolate and 1-1/2 oz. un-sweetened chocolate. Or you could use 6 oz. of 60% chocolate.
- 6 oz. unsalted butter at room temperature
- Pinch of table salt and 1/4 tsp. cream of tartar (for egg whites)

Egg yolks and sugar-preliminary blending: Separate the yolks from the white of the the eggs, dropping the white from the eggs into a glass (one at a time) and then into a stainless bowl. I say "one at a time" because, if you initially put all the white into the same bowl, you risk ruining the whole batch if you get even a tiny speck of yolk in the egg whites. Also, it is easier to separate the yolk from the white when the eggs are cold. Put the yolk into the stainless steel pan. (it's okay to get egg white in the yolk). Set whites aside. Using portable beater, beat the yolks for 2 to 3 minutes until pale-, lemon colored, and thick. This prepares them for being heated. You are now ready for the sugar syrup.

Set the pan with the coffee and water over high heat, blend in the sugar and bring to a boil, swirling pan by its handle. Let boil a minute or two until sugar has completely dissolved. Liquid will be clear. Immediately, bring the hot liquid over to the egg yolks; begin beating the yolks at moderate speed while you slowly dribble the hot syrup into them. If you rush this step, you will end up with scrambled eggs. Then set this aside while you prepare the chocolate for melting.

Melting the chocolate: Stir the liqueur into the now empty sugar-boiling pan (or in my case) double boiler (with water in the bottom). Cut the chocolate into slivers by cutting cross the chocolate $1/4$ inch or less at a time. One of my Editors uses a vegetable peeler. Place the slivered chocolate into the pan or double boiler. Cover and let the chocolate melt. Do not overcook. Check it often and stir it to help the melting process along. When you think it isn't quite all melted, take it off the heat and stir and stir and stir. When completely melted, set it aside.

Egg yolks and sugar-thickening over hot water: Set the egg-yolk pan over the second pan of water, and keep water at just below simmer. Beat the yolk mixture rather slowly but continuously with portable mixer for 5 minutes or longer, until it doubles in volume and becomes a thick cream that is quite warm to your touch. When warm and thick, place the pan into a large bowl of cold water and beat at moderate speed for 5 minutes or so, until cool. When you lift a bit on a spatula, the egg yolks should dribble off in a thick ribbon that takes several seconds to dissolve and absorb back into the surface of the main body.

Combining egg yolks with melted chocolate and butter: Stir the chocolate to make certain it is smooth and shiny. Remove from the hot water. Cut butter into 1-inch pieces and beat it rapidly, piece by piece, into the chocolate using the portable mixer. Scrape the chocolate into the egg yolks, then combine the two with a rubber spatula by cutting straight down through the center with the edge of the spatula, drawing the spatula to the edge of the pan, then bringing it up the surface in a scooping motion. (her definition of folding, really). Continue thus, rotating pan and scooping rapidly until the yolks and chocolate are fairly well combined, about 30 seconds. They will be mixed again later so don't over do it.

Beating the egg whites: At once before the chocolate and butter have time to cook and thicken, get to the egg whites. Question: Can you use your stand mixer for this step? Answer: absolutely. They must be at room temp. Being sure your beater is perfectly clean, whip the egg whites at medium speed for a minute until they are broken up and foaming. Add the salt and cream of tartar, and gradually increase the speed to high over a period of about 1 minute. Continue beating until the beaters leave definite traces in the egg whites, then begin testing. Egg whites should form stiff shining peaks. When lifted in the wires of the beater, just the tops of the peaks should bend down slightly. If you over beat, the egg whites will get grainy...not good. Just add another egg white and beat some more if this happens.

Completing the mousse: Immediately turn one fourth of the beaten egg whites out on top of the chocolate with your rubber spatula; scoop and fold in rapidly to loosen the chocolate mixture. Pour the rest of the egg whites on top, and rapidly fold them in, just as you combined the chocolate and egg yolks. Rotate the pan as you go (if you remember). The whole process should not take more than a minute. Remember, you are trying to deflate the egg whites *as little as possible.*

The mousse is now finished. It only needs to be chilled.

My favorite way to serve it is to spoon it in into an attractive bowl or individual serving glasses, cover and chill at least 4 hours or overnight.

It will keep for 3 to 4 days in the fridge. It can also be frozen.

You absolutely will never forget this mousse because it will be the best mousse you will ever eat. A lot of work? Yes, but not difficult work. Once you learn how to make it, you will have mastered many basic cooking methods that are used for many, many different dishes. And you will truly understand the egg and all its nuances.

Go ahead.
Try it. Now.

And since we aren't sure which came first, we must now address the chicken. First and foremost, don't buy a mass-produced chicken. The raisers of these chickens treat them inhumanely. Chickens don't deserve that. Some might suggest that chickens don't deserve to be killed either, but that's not the book I am writing. Instead, buy your chicken from a good source. A source that lets them roam. And a source that doesn't pump them full of chemicals. Free range, antibiotic-free chickens are good. An adequate product. Not perfect, but adequate. Again, I state my position based on the book Omnivore's Dilemma. If you don't have a local source, and hen houses are verboten, perhaps you can order chicken frozen and delivered to you. I found these sources on the internet in January, 2023.

- Thrive Market Organic chicken
- Crowd Cow Organic, pasture-raised chicken
- Cooks Venture Animal welfare-certified, heirloom chicken
- D'Artagnan Organic, certified-humane and pasture-raised chicken

I'm going to address chicken in another chapter so I will only say that a perfectly roasted chicken is a revelation. So simple. So quick (aside from the oven time). So good.

Buy yourself a good chicken. Then roast it.

There are plenty of recipes out there. My favorite is to salt the bird with kosher salt both inside and out. Use about 1 tsp. per pound. If you plan ahead, salt the chicken and stick it in the fridge for a day or two uncovered. This will dry the skin out which will result in a crispier bird.

A postscript mid-book:

Estero Bay and Morro Rock, Highway 1, California

Do not cook any egg on high in a skillet unless you want leather eggs. If you are scrambling your eggs, do it over very low heat, stir while cooking the entire time, and you will love the eggs. They will be soft as clouds. They will be a complete stranger to the eggs you get at Denny's, or the eggs you used to cook. It can take up to 10 minutes but the difference is earth shattering.

Roast Chicken

INGREDIENTS:

- 1 whole chicken
- 1 lemon
- Olive oil
- Salt and pepper to taste

Pair with 2022 Dresser Winery Sigh-La

DIRECTIONS:

Before cooking the chicken, take the chicken out of the fridge and let it come to room temperature (about 45 minutes). This methodology is under scrutiny, so do it however you want.

Preheat the oven to 425 degrees F. While the oven is heating up, smear some olive oil over the chicken and then apply salt and fresh ground pepper all over the outside.

Obtain a fresh lemon and wash it. Poke holes in it with the tines of a fork. Place the lemon in the chicken. Some folks truss the legs. I don't. In my opinion, trussing does not facilitate the cooking of the leg/thigh. I just let my chicken sit in the pan with its legs in a "natural" position. Place the chicken breast side down on a rack and place the rack in a low-sided pan (1 or 2 inches) so that the air can easily circulate around the bird.

Cook for 30 minutes. Then open the oven and flip the bird onto it's back for the final cooking. It takes about an hour. Because chicken is known to carry salmonella, I always use my insta-read thermometer to verify that the thick parts of the breast and thighs register 165 degrees. Once the chicken is removed from the oven, it's temperature will continue to rise. Things keep cooking after they have been cooked in the oven or on the barbie.

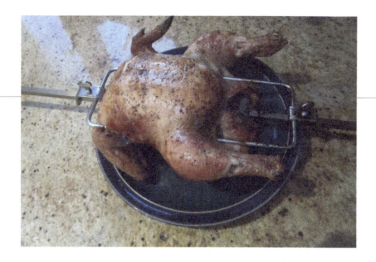

Then remove the chicken from the oven, turn off the oven, and tent the chicken loosely with tin foil, and let it rest for 20 minutes. Almost no one does this and it is very important. Cut too soon, the chicken's juices will vacate the bird leaving the poor chicken a bit dry. Better to let it rest so that the juices stay in the chicken's meat guaranteeing a moist and flavorful chicken. I cannot overstate the importance of doing this.

Let your bird rest!

You can barbecue or rotisserie the same chicken with few modifications. We use a Weber with a natural fire and it is great… rotisseried or simply placed on the grill with a drip pan on the bottom of an indirect fire. Actually, you need a drip pan when you rotisserie as well. If you aren't scared of fat, you can add potatoes or other root veggies to the pan and they will benefit from those chicken drippings.
There are so many recipes out there for chicken. If the chicken is good chicken, you simply cannot beat a simply cooked one. It's a revelation.

One other point. If you are in a hurry, this recipe will work without the pre-salting. It just won't be quite as crisp, but many people don't eat the skin so in that case, what the heck!

F is for Finger Food

I have a love-hate relationship with appetizers. The first thing about them is that they can ruin the appetite which is 180 degrees out from what their name implies. How many times have you gone to a dinner party where extravagant appetizers were served, only to take your seat at the dinner table stuffed to the gills? So, may we agree that appetizers really don't live up to their name?

Appetizers that are offered up often times come from the refrigerator case of Trader Joe's. Or they are made with "manufactured" food like bottled salsa, frozen guacamole, or that ubiquitous onion dip and chips. These are not good for anyone. My quest for real food continues, and food that is processed just doesn't fit the bill. It is high in sodium, preservatives, chemicals whose names are unrecognizable. And that doesn't even include all the hydrogenated oils and sugars with about fourteen different titles.

Really, people. You must consider the health risks associated with serving this stuff. There is a risk. I don't want to be the fresh food Nazi. Sometimes we are driven to short cuts and prepared foods. Okay. I'm off my high horse now. But you get the drift.

There are many ways to present a good appetizer that doesn't ruin one's appetite. How about carrot sticks? Oops. Carrot sticks that you personally cut up from fresh carrots. Not those carrot nubs that are packaged…so called "baby carrots." Those nubs are manufactured. They may enjoy a chlorine bath in the process. I didn't realize that bathing vegetables in chlorine is legal. But it is. No law against it. The idea of eating vegetables that have been washed and/or soaked in chlorine is unappealing. So, don't use those things for appetizers or anything else that I know of. Instead, a small dish of nuts (unsalted, or not). Some cheese. Feta with honey poured over. And, perhaps some cracked pepper to boot. Or, one of my favorites… Stuffed dates which I mentioned earlier in the date chapter. One other note about the nub carrots. It takes a zillion gallons of water to shape these darlings. Water we don't have.

In my kitchen, finger food includes licking the beaters. Who doesn't lick the beaters? I'm not talking about a boxing match here. Cookie dough is particularly good on those beaters. And, I think I am within my rights to point out that cookie dough made with flour, sugar, eggs, vanilla, perhaps some baking soda or baking powder qualifies as truly good, lickable food. Running the finger along the wire of the beater to get all that good goo off is a sinful delight. And fun. And I only lick beaters that have beaten home made cakes. I shun cake mixes. They are, well, manufactured. Throwing a cake together is not hard. It takes a few more minutes. But those minutes are well spent because they will make you a healthy and much more delicious cake!

Does the term "finger licking good" have any meaning to you? Silly question. However, there are so many things that are that good. Baby back ribs are that good provided the barbecuer (the only way to cook ribs is to grill them) hasn't burned them to a crisp. When I mention barbecue, I mean cooked over real fire. Those gas grills are convenient. However, you might as well just cook your food in your oven. Gas grills cook okay but the food that comes off the grill does not come close to the real deal. You can slather the meat with every concoction know to man but the meat will be lacking the flavor it would otherwise have had it been cooked over an open flame. A real flame.

But I digress.

Food grilled over a real fire can be burned. Care must be taken. Patience must be employed. Most people throw the food on way too early. When fire flares, the food may be ruined. A whole other topic, but a very important point to be made. Finger licking good does not include burnt to a crisp food.

Okay. So baby backs. What else? Chicken. Chicken needs to be picked up to eat it properly, with the exception of the breast. Chicken legs and thighs come to mind. Forget that old, white, boring breast. I advocate you stick with the bone-in legs and thighs. There are exceptions, of course. Stewed chicken. Chicken fricassee. Chicken that has fallen off the bone. But, you get the idea. Baked, broiled, barbecued. Pick up that chicken part and indulge. And then lick your fingers. And gnaw on that bone if you must.

Next is my favorite chicken recipe. Grilled, of course. Over a real fire.

Achiote Chicken

INGREDIENTS:

- 1 cut up chicken or some chicken legs and thighs. Your choice. I like the chicken parts.
- ⅔ c. freshly-squeezed orange juice
- ¼ c. anchiote paste (found in Mexican markets or on-line) Buy the rojo or red variety.
- 2 jalapeños, stemmed and seeded, or to taste. I recommend that you always test any chili pepper to gauge the heat and adjust the amount you use accordingly.
- 7 garlic cloves peeled and green core removed, if present.
- 1 Tbsp. black peppercorns
- 1 Tbsp. kosher salt
- 1 bunch of cilantro, washed and spun dry (stems included)

Pair with 2022 Dresser Winery Viognier

DIRECTIONS:

Make the marinade. Throw the orange juice, the paste, peppers, garlic, pepper and salt into a blender or food processor. Puree. Add cilantro and puree until smooth. Best if done a couple hours or a day ahead. I like to marinate the chicken overnight for maximum flavor.

Pour over the chicken, cover and refrigerate. Take the chicken out of the refrigerator at least 1 hour before cooking (aka bring to room temperature). Or not. Again, seems the whole "bring it to room temp" is being challenged as not necessary. So just do whatever you want.

Grill and enjoy. This is so good that I have a hard time doing chicken any other way. Take that as a warning and an endorsement!! And do not substitute pasteurized orange juice from the supermarket. Use the real deal. It isn't that hard to squeeze oranges, for heaven's sake. I find it useful to delegate squeezing to my sous chef, the Rayman.

Adapted from the *Two Hot Tamales* cookbook authored by Mary Sue Milliken and Susan Feniger.

Rayman does the Q in France

But, back to finger food. Other finger food includes but is not limited to croissants, doughnuts (Who eats doughnuts anymore?), sushi.

On **sushi**. Am I the only one who has tried to eat a California roll with chopsticks? It is impossible. Or, is it that I don't know what I'm doing? The roll falls apart. It is too big for one bite. What should be done? Pick it up and eat it. Then lick your fingers.

Much fruit qualifies as finger food, doesn't it. A peeled **orange**. A peeled **banana**. An **apple**. A **pear**. Anything you can hold in your hand easily qualifies here. After the treat has been consumed, a finger licking is entirely appropriate in my opinion. A mango doesn't qualify. A pineapple, no. Although, with a pineapple, if it is cut into manageable pieces, is quick and easy to eat with your fingers. And the list goes on. And the list includes tomato.

A dripping tomato on a BLT. Heaven.

Nuts. Especially salted ones are good candidates.

OMG. **Ice cream cones**. Invariably they drip. And it gets on your fingers with any luck at all and, voile, you have a lickable moment. So tasty. And as long as I'm on the ice cream subject, I have my favorite ice cream. And I'm contradicting myself here. Ice cream is manufactured unless made at home. So, I do take exception to my very own rule. However, some are more manufactured than others. You can seek out good ice cream that is only comprised of egg yolk, sugar, cream, flavoring such as vanilla, chocolate, salt, etc. Haagen Daz is one brand that makes the stuff. Look for local artisans in your neck of the woods. You may find one that makes good, pure ice cream. And if you can't, then Haagen Daz is a good way to go. Ben and Jerry's makes good ice cream. Probably a few things in it that break the rules. But, hey, the world ain't perfect and neither am I. Just remember, lick those fingers.

Toast. Who doesn't lick their fingers after eating a piece of toast? Toast and real, unsalted butter. Yummy. Or toast and butter and jam. Or toast and butter and egg yolk residue. The possibilities are huge. A toasted PB and J. A toasted egg salad sandwich. Yummy all. My grandmother served toast with ice cream. It made sense. Bread is cake without a sugar (usually) and with yeast (usually). They went together. Try it. You might like it.

Bacon is another food stuff that begs to be picked up and gobbled up. And that bacon grease? Heaven when licked off your fingers.

Fish and chips. All of it eaten out of hand, so to speak. Shrimp can be picked up by the tail and inserted into the mouth. And then licked off the fingers.

You notice, I'm not mentioning hot dogs, corn dogs etc. Manufactured. Don't do it. But hamburgers? Of late, I don't choose hamburgers much any more. Just lost my enthusiasm. But on occasion, I do like a great burger. If it isn't great, why bother? Which brings me to a funny story.

The L.A. Times has always been around. My grandmother had it delivered every day to our house on Oak Street in Paso Robles when Paso Robles, California was a dusty farming town of about 5,000 people. She was quite cosmopolitan in her small town life. And she clipped recipes out of the L. A. Times. Sometimes, she used her pinking shears. Nice touch. Sometimes, she just sort of tore them out. And then she would stick them in cook books, in drawers. Wherever. Often times she would use a straight pin to attach them to a page in a book. She took a deep interest in cooking.

So, when we moved to the central coast of California over the hill from Paso Robles, I ordered the L.A. Times. And Wednesday was my favorite day because of the food section. Loved the food section. Well, one year the L.A. Times decided to find the best burger in greater Los Angeles. Because the L.A. basin is one of the biggest consumer markets in the world, I figured the burger would be one of the best in the world also. So, when the Times tried to re-create the burger they liked, I decided I must try that recipe. But, first I had to try that hamburger. Which I did. It took us three times to find the restaurant open (it's in Santa Monica about 240 miles south of where I live.) When it opens around 3 p.m., a line forms down the block. Obviously, I was not the only one that read the L.A. Times.

But I am quite sure that we were the only people in San Luis Obispo county that drove down on three separate occasions (on business) and went by there to have their burger. Twice, they were closed. We were too early one time, and they were just closed the second. But we were motivated. The burger was fabulous. So I had to make it. And we did, for a party of 12. But here's the thing. The recipe called for ground aged beef. OMG. Aged beef. And two types of aged beef. Strip and ribeye steaks. Aged. Ground up. So, off we went to the Whole Foods market in Pasadena. When the fellow behind the counter asked me what I wanted and I told him, he said, "You want me ground up these steaks? Really?" He was incredulous. I figure I'm probably the first person who had ever ordered this, seeing as how aged beef costs about $25/pound. Maybe $32. Don't know. But when we left Whole Foods with my meat in a bag meant to keep it cool, I was about $110 lighter. And I blame it all on the L.A. Times.

To conclude, we fed 10 of our friends these fabulous grilled burgers. All decked out with blue cheese, Gruyere cheese, caramelized onions, balsamic vinegar, Worcestershire sauce. And bacon. And arugula of the baby variety. We all licked our fingers. My editor recalls that I also may have made the buns. This, I have done before so it is within the realm of possibilities.

Another finger food that rates mentioning is **focaccia**. While a bit labor intensive and time consuming, it is worth the work and the wait. I highly recommend that you try it sometime. It takes about 5 hours total spread over two days.

Focaccia Discussion

Essentially, you make a starter. A starter is a bit of yeast, some water, and flour. All you do is mix it up and let it grow over night. Then add to it more ingredients. Knead it in your heavy-duty mixer Let it rise. Punch it down. Let it rise again. Throw it in a cake pan with some olive oil. Decorate it with goodies. Shove it in the oven. Focaccia is your reward.

Transfer the focaccia to a cutting board. Halve the focaccia using a long knife; then cut one-half into 4 wedges (don't cut the other half until you are ready to eat it).

The photo is focaccia I baked with olives and mozzarella cheese. But, here's the deal. Find a recipe you love. I'll direct you to Nancy Silverton. She has books. There are newspaper articles about her and her recipes. It is complicated, more than say, a roasted chicken, so I'll leave it to the expert bakers to provide the instructions.

G is for Glorious Garlic

Imagining life without garlic is a stretch for me. And probably you too, unless you are allergic to the allium sativum, the scientific name.

Garlic is related to chives, to leeks, to onions to name a few in the genus. Beyond that, garlic is as indispensable to the cook as is onion. They often go hand in hand and pan to pan!!

If you want to consider this for a moment:

Garlic was found in King Tut's tomb. Closest pic I have of that from the period!

Garlic has lots of sulphur going on.

Garlic breath is somewhat neutralized with parsley and that is why parsley is often in the same recipe with garlic. Think Italian food.

Garlic originated in the Middle East by some accounts.

So now you have some of the interesting tidbits re: garlic.

My kitchen always has garlic in it. It's like bread and butter for many people. Can't live without it. So, rather than pontificate, a few garlic recipes will do the talking for me.

Roasted Red Potatoes with Garlic and Rosemary

INGREDIENTS:

- 1-1/2 to 2 lb. of red potatoes, cut into 1 in. pieces or so
- Garlic cloves to taste (I like about 8-10) smashed but unpeeled
- A couple of rosemary twigs, needle-like leaves torn off, or as my editor mentions, "Chopping the leaves imparts more flavor."
- Salt and freshly ground pepper to taste
- 2 Tbsp. olive oil
- 2 Tbsp. unsalted butter

Pair with 2021 Dresser Winery Daydream

DIRECTIONS:

1 Wash and cut up potatoes and put in a baking dish. Rip the leaves from the rosemary twigs and put them in the baking dish. Salt and pepper the potatoes. Put in the olive oil and the butter and make certain all potatoes are covered with a bit of the oil so they don't stick while baking. Amounts of oil and butter are guesstimates. You can also leave out the butter, if you wish, for dietary reasons. The dish will still be good, just not quite as rich.

2 Cover the potatoes with aluminum foil and place in a 400 degree preheated oven. Cook for 30 minutes. Remove the foil and add the garlic to the mix and stir to coat with oil/butter mixture.

3 Continue to cook for another 30 minutes or until the potatoes have a nice crust on them and can be pierced with a fork easily.

ONE NOTE:
You can also steam them for about 15 minutes to shorten the baking time.

There has be a resurgence of Brussel sprouts in the last couple of years and they are divine with garlic. Take a look.

Brussels to Love

INGREDIENTS:

- 1 pint Brussel sprouts (about a pound) rinsed
- 4 to 6 Tbsp. olive oil, to coat bottom of pan
- 5 cloves garlic, peeled
- Salt and pepper to taste
- 1 Tbsp. balsamic vinegar

DIRECTIONS:

1. Heat oven to 400 degrees. Trim bottom of Brussel sprouts, and slice each in half, top to bottom. Heat oil in cast-iron pan over medium-high heat until it shimmers. Dry the sprouts with a paper towel to reduce splattering. Put sprouts cut side down in one layer in pan. Put in garlic, and sprinkle with salt and pepper.

2. Cook, undisturbed, until sprouts begin to brown on bottom, and transfer to oven. Roast, shaking pan every 5 minutes, until sprouts are quite brown and tender, 10 to 20 minutes.

3. Taste, and add more pepper if necessary. Stir in balsamic vinegar, and serve hot or warm. One note here. I don't use EVOO when I am cooking over flame or in the oven. EVOO is more expensive. If you want to use regular olive oil, go for it. I find it at Costco. While it used to be ubiquitous, it has been disappearing faster than our democracy.

Some of the simplest things are delicious.

I remember one time when *Gourmet* magazine was still in circulation. They did a special edition with recipes with very few ingredients. Brilliant.

Here is an example adapted from their recipe on the next page.

Adult Pimiento Cheese

INGREDIENTS:

- 2 large garlic cloves
- 1 2 oz. jar diced pimientos or your own roasted red peppers, diced
- 3 c. coarsely grated sharp Cheddar (12 ounces) or some other cheese that can be grated.
- ⅓ to ½ c. mayonnaise (=I love Best Foods or Hellman's, east of the Rockies).
- crackers
- toasted baguette slices
- crudites

Pair with 2020 Dresser Winery Kaia Lee

You will notice the garlic leads the hit parade in this very simple appetizer. Make some tonight. You will love it if you love cheese.

DIRECTIONS:

1 Force garlic through a garlic press into a large bowl and stir in pimientos including the liquid in the jar. Add cheese of your choosing and toss mixture to combine well. Stir in mayo to taste and season with freshly ground black pepper.

2 Spread may be made 1 day ahead, covered and chilled. Bring spread to room temperature before serving. Serve with your choice of accompaniments. I like Wheat Thins. I love this with sharp or extra sharp Cheddar.

So, you are probably asking yourself, "What is green garlic?" It is young and immature and not as spicy or bold. It is essentially the garlic before it starts the process of developing cloves. It is used around the world but has just come to the attention of the USA. I never saw a green garlic until farmer's markets started to become popular. Leave it to the farmers to move us along in our enjoyment of juvenile veggies.

Spaghetti with Green Garlic

INGREDIENTS:

- Kosher salt
- 1 lb. spaghetti
- ⅓ c. extra virgin olive oil. Make sure it is EVOO.
- 3 heads green garlic, thinly sliced
- 1 Tbsp. chopped parsley
- Small pinch of red pepper flakes

Pair with 2021 Dresser Winery Tuscan Joy

DIRECTIONS:

1. Bring a large pot of salted water to boil and add the spaghetti. Cook until a minute or so before al dente, reserving 1 cup of pasta cooking water before draining. The pasta will continue to cook when you add it into the sauce.

2. Meanwhile, heat the olive oil in a large (3-quart) saucepan over medium heat until shimmering. Add the garlic, parsley, red pepper flakes, and ¼ cup of water. Cover and sweat, stirring occasionally, until soft, adding more water, if necessary, to keep the garlic from caramelizing too much.

3. Add the cooked pasta to the garlic mixture and toss well to combine. Add some pasta cooking water if necessary to bring the dish to a creamy consistency. Serve with more olive oil and the minced tops of the green garlic, if desired. Or add a bit of anchovy paste for an intriguing taste.

NIFTY TRICK:
If you need to peel lots of garlic, cut off the root end, separate the cloves, and then cut each clove in half. The skin will fall away, usually. As with anything else in life, some days it works; other days it doesn't. But try it. You might like it if it makes your day easier.

Recipe adapted from Alice Waters.

is for Herbs

Do you grow your own? If not, you might give it a try. Nothing quite like going outside, scissors in hand, to do some snipping. Rosemary grows like a weed, so even I can grow it. And so many recipes include rosemary, even cookies.

How about mint? Oh, Lordy, mint is a prized herb because like so many others, it is not savory. It is sweet and jazzy. It jazzes up drinks, lots of Middle Eastern food, iced tea, candy, drinks, ice cream. The list goes on. Mint also smells great and is used in aromatherapy these days.

When I was a kid, my Grandma Bird had a window air conditioner which hung off the house with the help of a wooden structure that kept it up in the air. There was a water spigot directly underneath the air conditioner, and that was a grand place for the growing of mint. The mint absolutely took over the entire area. It loved the dripping water from the air conditioner, which I guess, now that I think about it … it was a swamp cooler, of sorts. Anyway, my Grandma would ask me to go snip mint whenever she was making iced tea for dinner. Or when she was making fruit salad. Torn mint leaves on fruit salad is wonderful. Good for the breath too!

It goes great with fish, too. Here is a recipe on the next page that McPhee's shared years ago, adapted. McPhee's is a restaurant in Templeton, California. Great place.

Albacore Grilled with Mint Sauce

INGREDIENTS:

- 4 6 oz. albacore steaks or any firm white fish
- 3 Tbsp. (separated) fresh mint, chopped
- 1/2 c. extra virgin olive oil (you can use regular olive oil here)
- 1 Tbsp. fresh lime juice
- 1 Tbsp. red wine vinegar
- Pinch of kosher salt
- Fresh ground pepper to taste
- 1 Tbsp. fresh parsley or basil minced
- 2 shallots diced
- 6 Roma or the equivalent of cherry tomatoes, seeded and diced
- 2 cloves garlic blanched, then julienned*

Pair with 2022 Dresser Winery Viognier

DIRECTIONS:

1. Marinate albacore in 2 Tbsp. olive oil, 1 Tbsp. of the chopped mint and black pepper for 2-3 hours in the refrigerator.

2. In a glass bowl, mix remaining mint and olive oil with the last 8 ingredients. Taste and correct seasonings according to your taste.

3. Over medium-hot barbecue fire, cook albacore steaks to your own preference. Serve with mint

* Blanching is a process of scalding a fruit or veggie or herb in very hot water and then cooling it off in very cold water in an effort to reduce the loss of quality over time.

Along with mint and rosemary, some of my favorite spices* include cumin, coriander, and cardamon. They often show up together in many a recipe. They are the "Critical Cs" in my cupboard. I do not attempt to grow these. Better to order from Penzey's, on-line.

Cumin is the most used of the three. It's found in many cuisines around the world. Mexican cooking uses mucho cumin. It is an seed from an herb in the parsley family that everyone should have in their arsenal.

Coriander is a dried seed of the cilantro herb. Coriander loses it potency quickly so don't over-buy. One of the best things you can do with coriander or cumin is to put it in a pan and heat it up as that will bring out the aroma before you grind the spice up. Your diners will be very happy when then they find it in their food!! I cannot overstate the difference it makes to heat these seeds.

Another clue: If you don't have a grinder for your dry spices, invest in a coffee grinder. They are simple and easy to use. After you grind your spices (*Spices are related to herbs so I include them here because S is for Skeet and so, there you are), use a handful of rice to clean the grinder. Plop the rice in, give it a whirl, empty the rice out, then use a paper towel to wipe off the residue from inside the grinder, including the lid.

I read on Wikileaks that coriander was used in Coca Cola. That was news to me, but I'm sure it's true. It is also used to make certain beers and gin. I now understand why I like all that stuff.

One of Italy's favorite herbs is basil.

Since basil is one of my all time favorite herbs, let me tell you how I make pesto.

Inspiration for this recipe comes from Marcella Hazan.

Pesto

INGREDIENTS:

- 2 c. fresh basil leaves, tightly packed
- 1/2 c. of olive oil
- 3 Tbsp. pine nuts, lightly toasted in a small pan
- 2 garlic cloves, peeled
- ⅓ c. Parmesan cheese, freshly grated (parmigiano-reggiano)
- 2 Tbsp. pecorino romano cheese, freshly grated.
  (1/2 lb. to a lb. of pasta of your choice)
- Butter - two or three tbsp, softened to room temperature
- Hot salted water from the boiled pasta

Pair with 2021 Dresser Winery Cabyrah

DIRECTIONS:

1 Dump (a technical term) the basil, the olive oil, the pre-toasted pine nuts, and garlic into the Cuisinart or food processor of your choice. Let it rip until everything is soupy. Put it in a bowl and add the cheese, mixing it with a fork or spatula.

2 Fill the pot with water and salt generously, 2 Tbsp. Bring to a boil and add your pasta. Stir it to separate the strands or pieces of pasta. Cook until al dente, judging the cooking time given on the directions on the package. Reserve 1/2 cup of hot pasta water. Drain the noodles and then place them in a bowl. Smother the noodles with the pesto sauce and stir to combine. Tare or cut the butter into smaller pieces, add to the bowl and add some water (start with a few tablespoons and stir until the butter melts. Add more water if seems too dry.

3 Plate in a pasta bowl and serve with a baguette. It is so good. Enjoy!

NOTA BENE:

You could also just fish pasta out and put it in a single serving bowl if it's a night for the two of you just eating while watching the news.

 is for Ice Cream

It was a toss-up. Iceberg lettuce or ice cream. Ice cream won.

Who doesn't like ice cream? Perhaps your doc. Your doc may not like to hear that you eat ice cream daily. But, it can't be helped. If you like ice cream, then you love ice cream.

Most people buy their ice cream at the store. So do I. Although, I also have to admit that I own two ice cream makers because…I do.

My favorite ice cream maker is a Whynter. It is quiet, easy to use, and much, much better than Cuisinart. There are also other types of makers, but I like the ones that have a built in refrigeration unit. Hit go, and your ice cream gets churned until thick. Then, the only other thing required is putting it in the freezer.

As far as ice cream brands go, Talenti and Ben and Jerry's are good choices. And don't forget the local ice cream parlor if you have one in your area.

Besides just a scoop of ice cream on a cone, which is the very best way to eat ice cream in the summer, plopping a scoop or two in a glass with a generous pour of root beer is right up there as one of the world's finest treats. Everyone should have a root beer float at least annually. Make a point of it. And, again, you are welcome.

This is us eating gelato because we are in Italy. Gelato doesn't use as much cream as ice cream, but it is yummy.

Ice cream is frozen custard. Flan is a custard, not frozen. So, I thought it appropriate to share with you my travails of making a flan. The flan has eggs, but it also has caramel. And without further adieu, the story of my flan.

I am constantly amazing myself.

It started off as such a beautiful day. The sun was shining. We walked the dog and saw the seals frolicking in the bay. Oh, how lucky we were. I had a good feeling about the flan that I was assigned to make for a dinner party that night.

Admittedly, I've had nothing but problems with flans. This time it was going to be different. Really, flan? Why does this dessert elude me? It's the caramel; and specifically it is the transfer of the caramel into the pan. It is easy to screw up. First, the writer of recipes really can't be there to say, "Now. Take that sugar water that is about 1400 degrees (which is dangerously hot) off the burner and pour it into said pan and then roll the pan around so the caramel coats the pan everywhere, even up the sides of the pan." No. The writer of the recipe cannot be with you to tell you exactly when to take this action. And that seems to be the crux of the problem for me.

Now, knowing this in advance should aid me in the search of the proper flan. So, what did I do? Well, I picked out a recipe that really couldn't be much more difficult. In fact, it was maybe the most difficult flan recipe ever. In my own defense, it just looked so interesting.

But I digress.

So, I made the custard. No big deal although the non-cook may not appreciate the finer points of custard making. The most important thing to know is that you cannot add eggs into hot milk. The heat will cook the eggs and you'll end up with clumps of eggs. Ugh. You must whisk the eggs to "heat-proof" them. I did this and thus avoided the only mistake one can make with custard. Oh, except that I didn't have any vanilla beans and the recipe called for a vanilla bean. So, I substituted vanilla paste. It was then time to make the caramel.

The recipe I chose included annatto seeds. OH, and the recipe also called for 12 ramekins as each was to hold 4 oz. of custard. So this meant I had to not only know when the caramel was ready, but I had to pour the caramel into 12 separate dishes.

WHAT WAS I THINKING?

What happened was that the annatto seeds turned the sugar water reddish thereby making the decision of when to remove the caramel from the heat all the more difficult. That is because as the sugar water cooks, it turns auburn-colored. Then, the annatto seeds needed to be removed which meant straining the caramel through a strainer into each cup. OMG. I ended up with spots of varying shapes on the bottom of each cup. They resembled Rorschach tests. Elephant? Rabbit? Richard Parker? And there were drips of caramel all over the stove, and all over the pan for the bain marie. The kitchen looked like a cyclone came through.

Oh, the bain marie. That's a fancy french term for water bath. You put the cups in a pan and then fill the pan with water about half way up the side of the cups. And if that's not difficult enough, you cover the whole affair with tin foil and bake.

Let me digress.

I could not leave each cup with it splotches of caramel, so I put each cup over a flame on the stove until the heat caused the caramel to move. And then I picked off the caramel that stuck to the inside of each cup. It was at this point that I just knew my friend, Pat, really didn't like me. Why? Because she is the one that asked me to make the flan!!

The recipe writer reported that this recipe would make 12 servings. Fat chance. It made 7. So much for saving the extra custard for ice cream which the recipe writer suggested in the event of too much custard.

I think I will send the recipe writer a bill for the tea kettle. I emptied my tea kettle of water into the pan for the bain marie and then placed the tea kettle back on the stove. It was daytime. I could not see the flame, and these new fangled appliances do not indicate if a gas burner is on or not. So, it is not entirely my fault that I almost incinerated the empty tea kettle. What else could possibly go wrong?

J is for Jalapeños

Hot, hot, hot. If you don't believe it, just cut one open, touch the seeds or inside lining and then stick your finger in your eye. No, no. Don't do it unless you are masochistic. It will require you flooding your eye with water, possibly a trip to the emergency room...it is that bad.

Let me explain. As people get older, their taste buds calm down. I think this is why we like onions when we get older. It's why we like pungent cheese when we get older. It's why children don't like these things, generally speaking. This also explains why salsa has overtaken catsup as the favorite condiment in the 21st century. Having said this, people, it is important to learn how to handle peppers that are hot. They are an important part of your new-found love for heat.

For those that don't like heat or spice, I'm sorry. You may skip this portion.

Jalapeños are not the hottest peppers, but they are plenty hot. When cooking with them, it is a good idea to taste a bit to check out the "fire factor" (a technical term). Then you can decide how many to put in that guacamole. Or pico de gallo. Or whatever you happen to be making.

Next is a recipe I discovered years ago somewhere… around Thanksgiving time. I'm thankful I found it because it is delicious.

Roasted Cranberry Sauce

Here is a picture of the sauce before it went into the oven.

DIRECTIONS:

1. Heat oven to 450°. Using a peeler, remove peel from the orange, taking off as little of the white pith as possible. Cut peel into very thin strips about 1 1/2" long. Squeeze juice from the orange; strain and reserve 1 Tbsp. juice.

2. In a bowl, combine peel, cranberries, sugar, olive oil, salt, cardamom pods, cloves, cinnamon, and jalapeños. Toss and transfer to a parchment paper–lined baking sheet. Roast until cranberries begin to burst and release their juices, about 15 minutes.

3. Transfer cranberry mixture to a bowl; stir in reserved orange juice and port. Let sit for at least 1 hour so that the flavors meld. Remove and discard cardamom, cloves, and cinnamon

INGREDIENTS:

- 1 orange, preferably Valencia because they are juicy
- 1 lb. fresh or thawed cranberries
- 1 c. sugar
- 2 Tbsp. extra-virgin olive oil
- 1 tsp. kosher salt
- 4 green cardamom pods, smashed
- 4 whole cloves
- 2 sticks cinnamon
- 1 small jalapeño, stemmed and thinly sliced
- 1 1/2 Tbsp. port

K is for Kitchen

Well, this was a no brainer. It beat out kiwi, kumquat (a good scrabble word once in a lifetime), kidney pie, kosher kool aid (an interesting combo!), kidney beans, kibble (for dogs) and the list goes on. If I wanted to add Japanese dishes, the list would explode. But alas, the word kitchen is just too sweet.

In many homes across the country and around the world, the kitchen is where the action takes place. People love to lollygag around the kitchen. It is comfortable and inviting, usually. Smells emanate from the kitchen and that draws people and pets into the room.

Some of my fondest memories are in the kitchen. When I was a youngster, my grandmother spent most of her day in the kitchen. That is where breakfast was served, and we all sat down together and ate around a table that took up most of the room. Yes, the kitchen was a room with a door. It could be closed off from the rest of the house. On one wall was a built-in ironing board. My grandfather sat with his back to the ironing board. My grandmother sat opposite grandpa, and the cupboards were behind her.

I sat between them, and my back was to the stove. The GE stove had a built-in "crock pot". Grandma used to cook the pink beans in the well. It was actually nifty. I loved that stove. It was all analog.

Why do the appliance makers today use digital for the dials on our stoves, ovens, refrigerators, washing machines? A survey, if taken, would show that people prefer analog. It's easy. You just turn the dial. There is no way to screw up by, say, setting the oven temp and then forgetting to press start as some appliances require. And who needs to know the time is 4:17? Isn't quarter after 4 good enough for most people in a home setting? We have gone off the deep end with this digital stuff. I mean, really, folks. Don't you miss the ease of use and quickness of analog?

I digress. Grandma made her pink beans, and we all loved them. See the recipe under B is for Beans, page 16.

Anyway, back to the kitchen table. Because the stove was behind me, I looked across the table and out the window which jutted out about about 5 feet. Inside that "nook" was the Singer sewing machine with the bird cage on top. My bird's name was Casper (named after the friendly ghost), and he was a mean parakeet. Used to peck hard if a hand was inserted into the cage... any hand... he was non-discriminating.

There was a door to the left of the nook. This is the door with a window in it through which my Uncle Ralph used to terrorize me when I wouldn't drink my milk. He'd put on a tin mask decorated like an American Indian and stand outside and make weird noises and threats. I still wouldn't drink my milk. It was too warm for my liking. And to this day, if I drink milk, it has to have ice in it. Does the term scarred for life have any meaning to you?

So, as you can see, my grandmother really did spend hours and hours in the kitchen because she also ironed and sewed there. She made me clothes on that treadle Singer sewing machine. She needed me to try on dresses turned inside out while she went about pricking me with straight pens as she fitted the clothes. We did all that in the kitchen too.

When she ironed, the board came down with the basket of pre-starched clothes covered in damp towels stored underneath the board. She'd warm up the iron and away she would go. To pre-starch clothes, she had to literally dip the clothes in a solution of water and starch. It was extremely labor intensive. And the clothes that were starched couldn't be allowed to dry out for fear of permanent wrinkles (I'm guessing here.). And there was no steam iron. It was hard work. That's where I learned to iron.

The other interesting thing that happened in her kitchen was that she washed my hair in the kitchen sink. I hated it at the time, but, oh, how I love these memories now. She used to catch rain water in a big white porcelain-lined bowl outside the kitchen window directly below a rain spout. Then, she would bring the water in and heat it up on the stove. That is what she used to wash my hair in. The rainwater often had leaves and sticks in it, but that added to the ambiance. At my age, around 9, I was embarrassed. My neighbor, Nancy who was 8...her mom didn't do that. No one else I knew did that. Why did my grandmother do it? Now I know that it was because she was born in 1898 and lived in rural California most of her life. Conservation was important before the water was dammed and saved. Her early married life found her on the family ranch, 6 miles from town. She never learned to drive a car even though she lived until 1992. Once she took driving lessons from Mr. Asa, the high school football assistant coach and driving instructor. That ended when she drove him into some lady's shrubs. Oh, and then there was the time that she backed out of the garage, lurched across the alley and hit a big oak tree. She then put the car in drive and lurched forward and hit a steel post that housed a guide wire that attached to the antenna of the neighbor's house. It was a very high antenna for TV reception, actually the tallest one in the entire town. This resulted in hundreds of dollars worth of damage to the car, and she never made it out of the alley. She stepped out of the car and never returned to the driver's seat again.

But I digress.

Busy am I creating my own history in kitchens. It's not hard to do, really... especially if you have a knack like me of losing focus and burning things including myself or talking while chopping... that has led to butterfly bandages and the like.

However, one of the wildest memories of my own kitchen was the time that we hosted an honest-to-goodness real, live cookbook author and chef who also happened to be a Zen Buddhist (and I only mention this because that was how our Zen Buddhist friends led the cook to us.) And our Zen Buddhist friends, Margaret and Bob, are very mild-mannered people who make you think of Zen when you meet them or maybe low blood pressure or maybe quayludes. I'm just saying, they are low keyed.

They arranged a cooking demonstration for interested parties who were willing to pay $75 for some cooking knowledge, and it just so happened that we had a good kitchen for demonstrating cooking (more on this later). So... the day came and there was a knock on the door. Margaret and Bob were there with our master chef in tow. He was very charming. They had just come from a meditation and everyone was, well, calm. It was early afternoon and so Bob and Margaret (B & M) had packed a picnic which was eaten on our living room floor around a square low-lying coffee table that rested on an area rug. Lunch was very good as only B & M could have made as they are very accomplished cooks. Anyway, after we dined, the chef said, "I need to take a nap. Do you have a place for me to do this?" A bit taken back, the Rayman directed the chef to a bedroom and gave him a blanket, and there he lie resting while the rest of us, B & M and Rayman and moi and, oh, yes, the chef's lady friend started sorting things out. Really, folks, have you ever had a complete stranger come into your house, eat lunch and ask for a bed for nap? It was to my way of thinking a bit unconventional but, hey, maybe this is what Zen Buddhists do?

After the chef came to, it got very busy. The menu he was demonstrating involved copious amounts of veggies that required, slicing, dicing, and mincing. So we all jumped in and started prepping. And then the "students" started arriving, some we knew and some were complete strangers, perhaps themselves practicers of Zen. Seemed like a fun group. So the chef demonstrated how he minced garlic.

Midway into the demonstration he announced that he forgot his bell. His bell, he explained, was used to gain attention because when he needed the floor, he needed a way to hush the masses so that everyone could listen and learn. Because we did not have a bell to ring, we agreed that he would raise his arms up in the air instead. Okay, we nodded. But the wine was flowing (only in the great room, he forbade it in the kitchen) in between the chopping and mincing and people were busy prepping. Oh, and the pizza dough was being made, and this required the chef throwing $1/4$ of a cup of flour here, a $1/4$ of a cup of flour there as though he were trying to skip stones on the water...you know, side handed, perpendicular to the counter so that the counter, the floor, and the students were covered with flour. OMG. Who was going to clean this up?

Just to back up a bit, this same chef had done a demo at someone else's house the night before where he had nearly amputated a finger while demonstrating his sharp knife but none of us knew this at the time because he did not amputate it as evidenced by the fact that the finger was still attached to his hand. Anyway, he described how personalities were like different materials and his personality was like steel, like a knife. In hindsight that was pretty funny.

Again, I digress. Mushrooms needed to be sliced and cooked on the stove top and the ovens needed to be turned on so that the pizza could be cooked. His lady friend was standing behind him, along with one of the students discussing how to get this done. "How do you turn on this digital oven?", one wondered out loud when his arms went up. "Maybe we should use two pans," the other stated and about that time the chef came unglued. He started jumping up and down while yelling, "**My... arms... are... in... the... air. When... my... arms... are... in... the... air, you... should... not... be... talking. You cannot... learn... what... I... know... unless... you... listen. Do... not... talk... when... my... arms... are... in... the... air!**" And the decibel level of his tirade was about 500 db. It seems like this scene lasted about 10 minutes because time just stood still. Most of us looked at him like he was crazy. Jaws dropped. The women behind him who were helping him prepare the food (one was a paying customer, remember) to their credit, took it in stride, turned to the stove and continued to cook those mushrooms. And then the chef continued his regular demonstration. Well, my husband, Rayman, and our friend, Maurice, were astonished. They were standing on the other side of the counter, in the great room drinking wine. The Rayman thought, "What should I do? He is in my home, I have a group of people, several whom I do not even know, who paid $75 to take this class. How do I handle this?" Luckily, he and Maurice just decided to drink heavily, and we somehow made it through the demo. After the demo was done, the food cooked and eaten, the chef and his entourage exited stage left. And, we all cleaned up our kitchen.

You... can't... make... this... stuff... up. Too funny. As a postscript to this story, I have not taken up Zen Buddhism. I prefer my happy pills.

 is for Love of Legs

It occurred to me that I love legs. This, of course, does not make me an exception. Many people love legs. For heaven's sake, men love legs. Think Betty Grable. Didn't she insure her sticks? Just wondering. Tables love legs...it gives them needed height so that we might stick our legs under the tables. Travelers love legs. Legs of a trip make the trip that can get you from a large airport to a regional airport. Wine drinkers like legs...the legs on the glass from the wine. A wine isn't given the time of day if it lacks legs.

The legs I love most are, well. I don't know. Duck legs, perhaps. That's what made me think of legs in the first place. I just made duck legs and they were exquisite. A picture may help illustrate. The plating could have been more elegant. However, that leg looks good!

Braised legs for this dish. Braised in port. The recipe called for Banyals which is a fortified wine from France that I didn't have in the "cellar", so I substituted port.

These duck legs were to die for... as the duck surely did. And we love, love, loved these legs served along side a parsnip and turnip gratin... essentially these two tubular veggies cooked in cream and thyme.

The recipe used was from Suzanne Goin's cookbook, *Sunday Supper at Lucque's*. This cookbook should belong in all serious cooks' libraries because these recipes cannot be be found online. And you can't read her comments about the recipes and cooking methods. It is a must-have.

However, I do not want to mislead the dear reader. I love leg of lamb, too. OMG. Lamb leg that has been seasoned with salt and pepper and studded with fresh garlic slivers is divine. Trust me. And cooked on the grill. It's also fabulous roasted in an oven, but I love it grilled over real charcoal and/or wood. Even wood chips soaked before using then tossed on the charcoal to create a flavorful smoke which the leg will pick up is a great method. Leg of lamb done medium rare is a wonderful thing. And it has an affinity with asparagus and mint..but not that dreadful mint jelly you buy in the store. That stuff is awful and should be outlawed. Real gourmands don't eat that kind of mint jelly.

A mint salsa would be fabulous. Any kind of mint condiment that is homemade would be a great addition to the meal. Leg of lamb has something in common with insects too as it can be butterflied. Okay, okay. Butterflied leg of lamb can be stuffed with all kinds of goodies. Or it can just be butterflied and seasoned with salt, pepper, and garlic planted (just like the un-butterflied edition) for faster cooking. The butterflied leg also gives the cook the ability to serve all different types of doneness so that guests may have their pick of rare to well done...check with the guests before cooking. It may be that everyone likes medium rare so you will want to keep your incinerating to a minimum.

Lamb legs also take well to marinating. Overnight. They are just so versatile. And they are much less complicated to cook than duck legs, generally. And marinating gives them wonderful flavor. So, as you can see lamb legs are luscious.

Then there are chicken legs..affectionately referred to as drumsticks. Who thought up drumsticks, anyway? Interesting name. Chicken legs are easy to eat with your fingers which put them high up on my list of favorite finger foods. And legs are connected to thighs and chicken thighs are meaty, and dark, and flavorful. The tenderloin, of the chicken leg, if you will. I guess thighs are heavy-lifter muscles, so they have lots of muscle which makes them so appealing. You can buy them skinned, deboned, or with skin and bone. There are recipes for chicken legs to meet any need when you include the thigh as part of the leg, and I do. Heck, my thigh is part of my leg...so the chicken is no different.

My favorite recipe for chicken legs is one that uses achiote paste as part of the marinade. I wrote about it earlier in appetizers. Achiote is a derivative of the annato seed. It is used in Mexican cooking, and that is where I found the recipe concept. In *Two Hot Tamales* cookbook. Once you have had this chicken barbecued, you will have reached the pinnacle of chicken eating. Forget that bland breast. The leg is where it is at and no more so than when marinated. Just plan ahead so the chicken has time to marinate properly. You will not be disappointed. Oh, and you get the paste in a Mexican market or mercado. It comes in a box.

Cape Teals (Ducks) in Kenya

Incidentally, don't be afraid to shop at Mexican markets. They are fabulous and you are missing a wonderful place to shop. You owe it to yourself to shop at a Mexican market. Often they have fresh baked goods, marinated meats and poultry, fresh masa, salsa that they make fresh every day. And it is fun to wander the aisles and look at all the things they sell, often at much better prices than the Albertsons or Ralphs or Piggly Wiggly. In cello bags instead of jars and half the price.

Mexicans really love fresh food. When they were building a house next door to us a few years back, all the framers for the house ate lunch by lighting a Bunsen burner and cooking up their meal right on the curb. It was amazing. Smelled great. So...follow their lead and shop where they shop. You will be happy you did.

Duck suffers from a bad reputation. Too fatty, they say. Not so, I say. And why is that?

Duck recipes that I use require duck parts. Breast. Legs. Thighs. Yes, they have fat but the real offender I've been told is that ducks have fat sacks. Avoid those and all is well.

There is another discussion we must have about ducks. I prefer ducks raised for their meat. The wild ducks are not my cup of tea. They are just too, well, wild tasting. They must eat strange stuff because wild ducks taste strange to me. But, that's me. If you love wild duck then you should eat wild duck. Not sure if my recipe will work as well, but go for it.

Probably the most famous duck is Peking. Just about everyone has heard of it. Few have eaten it because it takes days. I have a recipe for another type of Chinese duck that must be steamed, then air dried and then deep fried, not once, but twice. The chances that any of my readers would take on such a demanding recipe is just about nil. However, I do think I have a perfect duck recipe that any cook can cook with relative ease.

This duck recipe will wow you and your guests if you choose to invite

My fave duck recipe

NOTA BENE:
You must start this the day before. Do it. It's worth it.

Pair with 2021 Dresser Winery Cabyrah

INGREDIENTS:

- 6 duck legs
- 1 Tbsp. fresh thyme leaves, plus 6 whole sprigs fresh thyme (use less if dried)
- Zest of 1 orange
- 1 Tbsp. freshly cracked black pepper
- Kosher salt
- 2 1/2 Tbsp. extra-virgin olive oil
- 1 1/2 c. diced onion
- 1/2 c. diced fennel
- 1/2 c. diced carrot
- 1 bay leaf
- Freshly ground black pepper
- 2 Tbsp. balsamic vinegar
- 2 c. of port or other fortified wine. Suzanne Goin uses Banyuls from France. I adapted this recipe from hers.
- 3 c. of chicken stock (best if you make it yourself… I hardly ever do)
- 1/4 c. flat-leaf parsley leaves

1 Trim the excess fat from the duck legs. Season them with 1 Tbsp. thyme, orange zest, and cracked black pepper. Cover and refrigerate overnight.

2 Take the duck out of the refrigerator 1 hour before cooking. Season the legs on all sides with 1 heaping Tbsp. of kosher salt. Heat a large sauté pan over high heat for 2 minutes. Swirl in the olive oil and wait 1 minute. Put the duck legs in the pan, skin side down, and cook for 8—10 minutes, until the skin is deep golden brown and crisp. Don't crowd the legs. If your pan is too small to fit all the legs, brown them in batches. Turn the duck legs over, reduce the heat to medium, and cook for 2 minutes on the other side. Move the duck, skin side up, to a braising pot. (The duck legs should just fit in the pan.) Preheat the oven to 325°.

3 Discard half the fat and return the frying pan to the stove top over medium heat. Add the onion, fennel, carrot, thyme sprigs, bay leaf, and a pinch of pepper. Cook for about 10 minutes, stirring often with a wooden spoon and scraping up all the crusty bits. When the vegetables are browned and caramelized, add the balsamic vinegar and Port. Turn the heat up to high, bring the liquid to a boil, and cook for 6—8 minutes, until the liquid has reduced by half. Add 3 cups stock and bring to a boil. Turn the heat down to low and simmer for 5 minutes.

4 Pour the broth and vegetables over the duck in the pot, then scrape the vegetables that have fallen on top of the duck back into the broth. The liquid should not quite cover the duck. Cover the pan very tightly with aluminum foil. Braise in the oven for about 2 1/2 hours, until the duck is very tender. To check for doneness, carefully remove the foil and pierce a piece of the duck with a paring knife. If the meat is done, it will yield easily and be tender but not quite falling off the bone.

5 Turn the oven up to 400°. Carefully transfer the duck to a baking sheet and return it to the oven to brown for 10—15 minutes. Strain the broth into a saucepan, pressing down on the vegetables with a ladle to extract all the juices. Skim the fat from the sauce. Reduce the broth over medium-high heat, about 5 minutes, to thicken it slightly. Taste the juices for seasoning. Transfer duck legs to 6 wide bowls. Spoon the juices over the duck and scatter the parsley leaves over the top. Or dish up on a plate. Your choice.

I feel badly about eating ducks. They are sweet animals. And smart. We have ducks on our golf course and if you give them some stale bread, they will remember you forever. Quack, quack, quack. They are fairly fearless too. They come up pretty close for that food. Males and females alike.

Ducks are also responsible for duck hunters. And duck hunters are a strange breed. In California, we have duck clubs. Grown men pay a lot of money to belong to these clubs. Then, they get up really early in the morning, don camouflage clothes, grab their guns and their dogs and head for the blinds. There they sit in freezing water and wait for unsuspecting ducks. This is defined as fun. As I view it, it is akin to torture.

Really, folks. I prefer my method. I jump in the car, go to the store and buy ready-to-cook duck. Oh, I know. Where's the fun? I'll leave that to the guys. I suppose if you look at all the money it takes to be a duck hunter, you have to conclude that it is not a cost effective way of eating. Probably, they pay about $2,000 a pound when all is added up and divided by the number of ducks shot. Or more. Just saying.

Do yourself a favor and try duck today. You will not be disappointed. Those sweet little things are, unfortunately for the duck, very tasty.

Back to legs. Quail have legs. See my chapter on Q is for Quail. Turkeys have legs. Really, if you think about, animals legs are long on flavor and easy to cook. Who in the world doesn't like legs?

 is for Macarons

When the Rayman retired, we decided that travel was in our future. If not now, when? And one of the places that we wanted to go was France. Being interested in food made France a no-brainer. And the Rayman had studied French, the language, in high school and college so he was not completely uncomfortable with the notion of France. So, we booked a river cruise and took, as it were, our virgin voyage down the Soane and the Rhone. Fabulous. Except for the fact that we upgraded to a better cabin with a balcony so that moi could have fresh air at night. They don't call me the traveling princess for nothing. It turns out that the boat's motor was located at the back of the boat, and the boat was engineered so that the diesel fumes permeated our cabin. But, that's another story. What I really want to tell you about was our second trip to France, because we loved France so much we just had to return. And one reason that we loved France so much was because of its cookie, the macaron which I will expound on as this chapter unfolds.

Two things you should know. One is that to prepare for the second trip, we studied French on Rosetta Stone for 9 months fairly religiously. The other thing you should know is we traded our home with a French family through the on-line service called Homelink. Homelink is a website that you join for a price and it gives you access to other like-minded people who want to save money on travel by swapping houses. Of course, there are other benefits. One is that when swapping houses, you get to stay in a neighborhood rather than a hotel so you can meet neighbors, and go to the grocery store. Really, just experience life as the French do. It is wonderful. "Oh, how can you let someone else, complete strangers really, stay in your home?" is an often asked question? Well. Here's the thing. Our home is full of stuff. Their home is full of stuff. Chances are the stuff will be fine. And besides that..it's just stuff.

My dear Aunt Clover spent her life, as I saw it, taking extremely good care of all of her possessions. She loved her clover-leaf knickknacks we all bought her. She loved her glass double boiler. She loved her pictures of flowers that graced her walls. But when she got so old that she could not live without assistance, she ran an ad in the local newspaper, had a garage sale and what she didn't give to all her relatives, she sold. Just like that. So, I asked her how she could do that, and she said, "It's just stuff." And that is why we can do trades with perfect strangers. Remember, you own your stuff or your stuff owns you. Most people can't do it.

But I digress.

On our trip to France, we traded homes with a wonderful French couple and their three children, ages from 14-20. And that trip changed our lives completely because of experiences that I will detail here. What is recorded below is my actual impression of arriving in France as described in my travel blog. I write my travel blog because I can't remember sh_t. I mean, it is so bad, I have spent way too many hours (estimate) standing in my kitchen pantry wondering why I'm there. What did I go in to get? Some of you may relate to this phenomenon. So, because of this, I figured I had better write my stories down before I relegate my experiences to the dustbin of history. And so, here goes.

An excerpt from 2010.

"Well, we arrived. Late. But, nevertheless, an arrival. It is 2:50 a.m. and we're enjoying a glass of wine and some chocolate before Mr. J (Rayman, my husband) and I retire. It was, after all, a fabulous trip here aside from the time that Mr. J snarled at me in a rottweiler-kind of snarl. And aside from the time that I screamed, "Just pull over and look at the map!" as we got more lost by the second in gay Paree!! And then there was the episode of trying to pay the machine for the use of the toll road. Imagine, if you can, Rayman driving and pulling up to the the machine automatique to pay the toll for the short trip we took south of Paris to Orleans. It was like 11 euros. So, Rayman put the ticket into the machine and the credit card into the slot marked carte or card...and the darn thing spit them both out with an impressive amount of velocity. So much force that they hit the car and then hit the ground.

Well, Rayman was parked too close to the machine and he couldn't open the door. Tempers started rising in direct relationship to the frustration level. So, I hopped out of the Citron and ran around the front of the car. He was so close, I couldn't retrieve the items. Of course there was a car behind us...people waiting in the darkness of their car, no beeping, being mysteriously silent. So, I ran around the back of the car and crawled down to pick up the ticket and the credit card, and then I reinserted the ticket. I can tell you that it was a great relief to the Rayman that my attempt was no more successful than his.

So, desperate to free ourselves of more embarrassment, he fed a 50 euro into the machine. Well, you would have thought that you were at Las Vegas and had won the big grand slam. Euros just kept gushing and gushing. By this time, Rayman was screaming something like "these god damn euros just keep coming" as he heaved them by the handfuls into the car. Then he put the car into reverse, "God damn this car", and then righted himself by putting the car into forward and we pulled over to re-group.

There were a few more episodes that occurred before we arrived at our French vacation home... like when we could not find the street to turn on from the main drag. The French have a lovely, quaint habit of essentially hiding the names of streets on sides of buildings. Often, these words are on buildings that are hundreds of years old and so is the paint they use to "highlight" them. It is lovely when you are walking about. But when you are dead tired, with a snippet of moon and few street lights in a never-been-to before place, it is downright discouraging. But that's another story.

And that is how our first night in France played out.

Now, if we had taken a shuttle to a local hotel upon arrival, none of this would have happened. And that's really the point. If we had done that, I wouldn't have stories and memories nearly as rich as these.

Another adventure in France was when we went to the airport to pick up our son who was flying in for a week. For reasons I will explain, we decided to book an hotel near the airport so we could stay in Paris the next day and do some touristy stuff. And, it went something like this.

Don't you love those movies that begin in the middle or the end and work their way back to the beginning? Pulp Fiction comes to mind. Well, we had a Pulp Fiction kind of day in Paris.

As we were taking a bus back to the hotel at 12:30 a.m., we ended up having the only English language conversation of the day with a couple from Boston. How did we find out they were from Boston? Ray mentioned that one time he was kicked off a train in Boston because it was late and at the end of the line (but not quite where Ray wanted to go). The train just stopped. When he asked the train driver why he was stopping there, the train driver said, "If you don't get off this train, I'll call the authorities" in a proper Bostonian accent. The nice couple from Boston asked Ray if he had ill feelings about Boston. Ray assured them that he did not.

But, I digress. The nice couple from Boston told us about their day and how they spent much of it lost in Paris, waiting for a bus that never arrived, going the wrong direction etc. Their stories immediately put us in a mood of, well, vindication. Alas, we too had such a day all because of a need for a new pair of shoes, which we were told would be on sale.

So, we ended up on the bus in the middle of the night because we were on the train from Paris going back to the hotel near the airport. Only the train stopped several stations short of the airport and a nice man announced that it was the last station for the day. Well, deja vu all over again!!! Because we couldn't think of how to ask why this was so in Francais, we picked up my shoes and waddled off the train to a bus that was waiting for us nearby. And that's how we met the nice couple from Boston.

Now, all of that happened after we spent hours trying to find this RER train that stopped before we wanted it to...while we were in Paris. After purchasing the shoes, which I am actually almost mad about because they caused us much grief, we spent literally hours walking around trying to find a 1.) place to eat and 2.) the RER train. Why didn't we just look in our book to find a restaurant? Well, we left the book at the hotel. And that's not the half of it. Should I continue? I risk doing so because you might think we were ...well, I'll leave it at that.

Back to the search for the train. I convinced Ray that we should jump on the Metro (read "let's try to make this fun".), get off at an unknown station and see what we could find in the way of a restaurant. So, we approached the man behind the chain-linked booth in the Metro (their subway system in Paris) and told him our plans in Francais. He recommended a stop so we bought the tickets and walked to the platform. Only, we couldn't exactly remember the stop (it started with an M), and we didn't know if the approaching train would take us there. So we went back up and asked for directions. They gave us directions (in Francais) and we went back down to the platform, but we couldn't figure out how to get where we were going. And, in the words of Yogi Berra, "If you don't know where you're going, you'll wind up somewhere else." After much gnashing of teeth, we decided that by leaving the subway and going literally nowhere, we were better off than the alternative. So, we spent about 8 euro to wander around the station and then to leave from the same entrance we had entered, say about 45 minutes earlier. Getting lost can cost you time...and money.

But I digress.

I mean honestly. Has anything remotely like that ever happened to you? Well, if it hasn't happened to you, it did happen to the nice couple from Boston. And that made us feel a little better as I mentioned earlier.

Since my "plan" didn't work out so well, you can imagine Rayman's reaction. It wasn't pretty. So, I then put him in charge. He found a restaurant on a corner very close to Notre Dame called the Hunchback of Notre Dame's Bistro. Well, that may not be the exact name of the place, but it is very close if my memory serves me well. Oops, let's not go there.

So we had a surprisingly good dinner. Although, I was exhausted, my feet hurt (No, I was not wearing my new shoes.), and it was hot. Oh, and it was about 10:30 p.m. So, I just had a tomato tarte. And a copious amount of wine. When we finished eating, we asked for directions, this time in English. The waitress told us where to go...politely. We followed her directions but the entrance to the subway had a bright red light which we interpreted to mean "don't go in". So, we wandered around looking for another entrance. We turned a corner and there it was. The Notre Dame Cathedral sans the hunchback.

We searched and searched and could not find another entrance, so we stopped deux policiers and asked for directions. They told us to go to the entrance with the red light. We walked back and went down into the station but it was closed at the bottom by a chain link fence. Long story short, we asked a shop keeper on the street by the bridge over the Seine where the entrance was. He told us there had been a problem earlier and they closed the entrance. Best bet was to walk to another entrance which was the station that we had tried to ride to earlier for 8 euro. And that's how we found the train.

So, back to square one. We had journeyed up to Paris to pick up Ryan who was due to arrive by dawn's early light. Deciding to do the logical thing, we set out one day early with our guides de touristes in hand and a reservation for a room at a Novotel (big hotel chain in Europe) near Charles de Gaulle airport north of Paris. Novotel must be a huge chain because we found not one, but three of them near the airport. And, we found the first two before we found the one where we were booked. After driving in circles in roundabouts (literally), and taking several wrong turns, one which ended us up near a cornfield with no hotels in sight, we finally arrived. And that was how we found our hotel... which was perfectly located in the direct line of the flight pattern about 1000 meters from where all the planes touched down. But, that didn't matter much because we were in downtown Paris getting lost, and we didn't return until 1 a.m. And, the way we returned was on a shuttle (from the airport to the hotel) which we caught after we arrived at the airport on the bus from the train. Confused? So were we!!

Ryan, by the way, arrived and spent most of the day doing Napoleon's tomb (above), the military museum and looking for a parking place.

"

I replicated the earlier potato recipe and voila. Here's the picture.

As you can see, we had many adventures and it was just three days into the trip.

The French family had a garden and our favorite vegetables to harvest and cook out of that garden were the potatoes. We did not fry them though. This is what we did, prose style. And, pardon my potatoes in the macaron chapter. Stream of consciousness, baby!! Harvest the potato. For city folks, that means go out with a claw-like tool and scrape through the dirt and find the potatoes. These were fingerling-type potatoes.

It's that easy. And the fresh potatoes are a revelation.

Here in America, our gas for cars and trucks is cheap compared to Europe. This is well known. And, in Europe, they have many more diesel cars than we do. Those two facts came together in one eventful afternoon that we shall not forget.

The recounting of the event begins:

" After we dropped off Ry at the train station for his trip home, we managed to navigate our way out of Dijon, the city of major street (rue) renovations. (We are sure CalTrans has moved part of their business off-shore.) We eventually found the freeway/toll highway. I was driving and Rayman was co-pilot. We needed petrol. So we exited and bought gas. As I was sitting there, Ray approached the car, white as a sheet. "I don't know if I bought the right kind of gas," he exclaimed.

Well, let me just say this. I'm a bit old and not as limber as I think I am. Climbing into the back seat of a tow truck is tres dificile (very difficult/hard). And not climbing into the tow truck was not an option. So, when we arrived at the garage, a VW dealership, I wanted to ask for a ladder so that I would not break something getting down.

You know, the car dealerships are much different in France. There were three cars in the showroom with trois (3) women, one in her own special room. To keep ourselves busy while they PUMPED the TANK empty of unleaded gasoline versus the diesel which we should have used, we looked at the autos for sell. No sticker is posted on the windows. No sales person rushing out to sell us a car. None of that. One woman behind the counter was dealing with another poor chap, and he didn't speak much Francais. He apparently had a burnt out lightbulb. Clarification. His auto had a burnt out lightbulb.

She had a skirt with an uneven hemline (think Tinker Bell), and stylish boots that came to just above her ankles. Her blouse was low cut, and she had a 3 or 4 inch thick belt that was positioned across her hips which were a bit generous, but not bad. Those boots did some walking. She kept stomping out of the showroom to the garage where our car was being DRAINED. She seemed angry. It took her and the garage men multiple trips to change the chap's light bulb. She seemed unhappy. He was unhappy. Rayman was beating up on himself for putting unleaded into a gas tank that only used diesel. And I was laughing. The scene was just too funny. That is until the bill came. $320. And that didn't count the gas we had to buy to fill up the tank again! Oh, and the unleaded we bought by mistake in the first place.

Now, the good news. We were smart enough to recognize the problem before we drove away and ruined the engine.

France was not without its difficulties, but it was so worth it because we got to eat macarons. Coconut comes to mind when macarons are mentioned. But the French make small meringue cookies called macarons. They are absolutely delicious and they are almost easy to make.

M is for Macarons, just as a reminder. Since you have read about eggs and egg whites earlier, I shall not hesitate to encourage the brave to try their hand at macaron making.

My macaron career started with the aid of *Fine Cooking* magazine. They did an article and this gave me the gumption to try my hand at these wonderful cookies. Every bite transports me back to France.

The recipe should yield about 30 macarons. More or less. Just depends.
Yields 30 to 36 1¾-inch sandwich cookies.

Macarons

INGREDIENTS

- 2 c. (8 oz.) powdered sugar
- 1-⅓ c. (4.5 oz.) finely ground blanched almond meal
- 3 to 4 large egg whites, at room temperature
- ¼ tsp. almond extract
- 3 to 6 drops of food coloring to match your flavor (optional), or in the case of chocolate, see additions listed under variations.
- ¾ c. filling, such as lemon curd, chocolate ganache, buttercream, chestnut spread, Nutella, peanut butter, or jam

FINDING ALMOND MEAL

If your local store doesn't carry it, you can find it on-line. It is worth it. Never scrimp on ingredients. It pays to go with the expert's recommendation.

DIRECTIONS:

Combine the powdered sugar and almond meal (almond flour) in a bowl and mix together thoroughly with a whisk or fork. Pass through a medium-coarse sieve (I use a strainer and tap on the sides to get the flour through.) to lighten and aerate the mixture which makes it easier to fold into the inflated egg whites.

In a glass measuring cup, add enough egg whites to reach halfway between the ⅓ cup and ½ cup mark; or use a scale to weigh out 3.75 oz. of egg whites. Transfer these to a large bowl, and save the rest for another purpose or discard. Actually, egg whites can be frozen.

With an electric mixer, beat the egg whites at medium speed until they form soft peaks when the beaters are lifted (See picture on p. 37); add the almond extract and the coloring, if using. Beat at high speed until the mixture forms stiff, but not dry peaks when the beaters are lifted.

Pour all of the almond flour mixture over the egg whites. With a large rubber spatula, fold the almond mixture into the egg whites just until it is fully incorporated. The egg whites will deflate somewhat, but the batter will be thick and moist and almost pourable.

Drop heaping teaspoons of batter 1 inch apart on parchment-lined cookie sheets. Or transfer the batter to a large pastry bag fitted with a 1/2-inch plain tip (Ateco #806 to #809) and pipe out disks in the following manner: Hold the bag vertical with the tip about 3/8 inch from the pan liner. Squeeze the bag without moving it until a disk of batter 1 1/2 inches in diameter is formed. Stop squeezing a second or two before moving the bag to pipe the next disk. Repeat, piping disks 1 inch apart.

Let the macarons rest for 20 to 30 minutes, or until the surface of the disks is ever so slightly dry. This crust will help form characteristic little "platforms" at the base of the macarons as they bake.

I really like the pastry bag method. If you don't have a pastry bag, you can put the batter in a plastic bag and snip the end of one corner about 1/2 inch from the end and pipe the batter out that way. Or, borrow a pastry bag from a friend!!

Meanwhile, preheat the oven to 400°F. Position racks in the upper and lower thirds of the oven.

Slide two sheets of macarons into the oven and immediately turn the temperature down to 300°F. Bake for 12 to 15 minutes, until the macarons are barely starting to turn golden (They will be golden on the bottom, though you will have to destroy one macaron to find out.) Rotate the pans from top to bottom and from front to back halfway through the baking time to ensure even baking. Set the pans or just the parchment paper liners on racks to cool.

When the cookies are cool, lift a corner of the parchment pan liner. Holding a cookie with the other hand, carefully peel the liner away from the cookie (Don't try to pull the cookie off the liner or you will lose the bottom of the cookie). Repeat with the remaining cookies.

Spread 1/2 to 1 tsp. filling on the flat side of a cookie and top with a cookie of matching size.

Voila. French macarons. Here are some variations:

Lemon Macarons: Add 1 tsp. of finely grated lemon zest and (if you insist) 4 to 6 drops of yellow food coloring just before the egg whites are fully beaten. Fill the cookies with lemon curd.

Raspberry or Strawberry Macarons: If you like, add 4 to 6 drops of red food coloring to the egg whites just before they are fully beaten. Fill cookies with raspberry or strawberry preserves, or any berry preserves.

Chocolate Macarons: Mix 3 Tbs. unsweetened cocoa powder (natural or Dutch-process) with the powdered sugar and almond meal. Fill cookies with chocolate ganache. Coffee Macarons: Add 1 1/2 tsp. instant espresso or coffee powder to the powdered sugar and almond meal. Fill cookies with coffee buttercream.

Happy baking and eating!! Oh, and don't get discouraged. My friend Nancy and I made these together the first time… and hers were much better looking than mine. She just had a knack. However, practice makes perfect, and as you practice, you will get better. Trust me.

If you fall in love with meringue, check out recipes for Pavlova, an Australian delight that makes a great presentation at a party. It is big, it is bad; it is boisterous.

There is one other dessert with meringue that is much easier and very good to serve after a heavy meal. I must include it too.

Angel Pie

DIRECTIONS:

Meringue

Heat oven to 275. Grease 8 inch pie pan/dish. Do a good job greasing because if you don't, the crust will stick to the pan/dish.

Beat egg whites on medium until frothy. Add cream of tartar and beat on high until soft peaks form. Gradually add 1 c. sugar and beat until stiff peaks form.

Ladle into pie pan and spread to edges.

Bake 55 minutes. Cool at room temperature. It will look like the picture below.

INGREDIENTS:

- 4 eggs, separated
- 1/4 tsp. cream of tartar
- 1 1/2 c. sugar (separated)
- 4 Tbsp. fresh lemon juice
- 2 tsp. water
- 1 c. whipping cream
- 1 Tbsp. lemon peel

Filling:

In small bowl, beat yolks until thick and pale. Gradually beat in 1/2 c. sugar then 4 Tbsp. lemon juice and 2 tsp. water. Pour into double boiler. Cook and stir occasionally until thick. Cool. Whip the cream. Fold the whipped cream into the cooled mixture. Pour into meringue shell. Refrigerate. Garnish with sliced strawberries or not.

N is for Nectarines

It was many years ago when my friend, Pat, was a member of our gourmet dinner group when we lived in San Ramon. We, Rayman and I, were both working for the phone company then, and we had become an item. So much of an item, that we bought a house together. And I turned into a domestic goddess in the kitchen. So, I formed a group of friends for eating and drinking. And Pat was bringing the dessert.

Dinner was at 6 p.m. At 7:00, still no Pat. So, I called, and she said she would be there just as soon as she finished the dessert. A nectarine mousse cake. If memory serves me well, I think she waltzed through the door about 8:30 with dessert. What a hoot.

We all agreed that the nectarine mousse cake was divine and worth waiting for, but, that it was very labor intensive. And so this story is a good way to highlight that there are easy recipes, and there are difficult recipes, and there are time-consuming recipes. This was difficult and time-consuming. On the next page, you will find the recipe.

Nectarine mousse: aka *Gateau Mousse a la Nectarine*

A French creation.

GENOISE CAKE

- 4 eggs
- ⅔ c. sugar
- ⅔ c. flour
- 1/2 tsp. salt
- 1 tsp. vanilla

In a metal bowl, whisk together the eggs and sugar. Make sure to whisk for 3 minutes to prepare the eggs for the heat. Don't want curdled eggs.

Then set the bowl on a pan of simmering water, and whisk mixture until it is warm and the sugar is dissolved.

Remove bowl from pan and, with an electric mixer, beat the mixture at moderate speed for 10-15 minutes or until it is triple in volume and cooled to room temperature. (I use an electric handheld mixer for the above process.)

Meanwhile, sift flour with salt onto a sheet of wax paper. As a reminder, always have wax paper in your kitchen. It is extremely useful.

In a bowl, combine the vanilla and butter. Sift and fold flour mixture into the egg mixture in batches until the mixture is just combined.

Stir a fourth of the mixture into the butter, and fold the butter mixture back into the batter.

Line the bottom of a buttered 8 1/2-inch springform pan with wax paper, or parchment paper and butter the paper, then dust with flour, shaking out the excess. I hit the pan on the kitchen faucet to de-flour the pan. A bit messy, but highly effective.

Pour batter into the pan, smoothing the top.

Bake in the middle of a preheated 350 degree F oven for 30-35 minutes or until a tester comes out clean.

Let the cake cool in the pan on a rack for 5 minutes, then remove the side of the pan, and invert onto the rack.

Remove paper and let cake cool

Nectarine mousse, continued

NECTARINES:

- 1 1/2 lb ripe nectarines
- 1/2 c. sugar
- 5 tsp. unflavored gelatin
- 1/4 c. fresh lemon juice
- 1/4 c. peach schnapps
- 1 1/2 c. heavy cream, well chilled

Halve, pit, and chop nectarines and, in a heavy saucepan, combine them with sugar and 1/2 cup water. Bring to a boil, stirring, and cook at a slow boil, stirring occasionally, for 15 minutes. In a food processor, puree the mixture and force it through a fine sieve into a large bowl, pressing hard on the solids.

In a chilled bowl, beat the cream until it holds soft shapes (not as stiff as soft peaks) and fold it into the nectarine mixture.

PEACH SYRUP:

- 1/4 c. sugar
- 1/3 c. peach schnapps or monin peach syrup

In a small saucepan, combine the sugar and 1/4 cup water. Bring to a boil, stirring until sugar is dissolved, and stir in the schnapps. Let the syrup cool to room temperature.

PEACH GLAZE:

- 1 1/4 tsp. unflavored gelatin
- 3/4 c. peach preserves or jam
- 3 Tbsp. peach schnapps or monin peach syrup

In a small saucepan, sprinkle gelatin over the lemon juice and schnapps, let it soften for 5 minutes, then heat mixture over low heat, stirring, until gelatin has dissolved. Stir gelatin into nectarine puree, blending the mixture well. Let it cool to room temperature.

ASSEMBLY:

Trim the Genoise and cut it into three layers, horizontally with whatever method you prefer. Some use dental floss, unflavored!

Center one layer in the bottom of a 9-1/2-inch springform pan and brush with half the peach syrup. Pour half the mousse over the cake and top it with another layer of genoise. Brush with the remaining peach syrup and pour the remaining mousse over the cake, rapping on the side of the pan to expel any air bubbles and smoothing the surface. Chill for 2 hours, or until it is set.

ASSEMBLY — PART DEUX:

Pour all but about 2 Tbsp. of peach glaze over top of the mousse cake, covering it completely, and chill the cake for 2 hours, or until glaze is set. While cake is chilling, in a food processor, grind the remaining genoise layer into fine crumbs. Toast the crumbs in a jelly-roll pan in a preheated 350 degree oven for 5-8 minutes or until they are golden. Reserve.

Cut half the nectarines into thin slices, and arrange them decoratively on top of the cake in a pinwheel pattern. Brush the remaining glaze over the nectarine slices and chill the cake, covered, for 1 hour, or until the newly-applied glaze is set.

Run a thin knife around the edge of the pan and remove the side of the pan. Working over a sheet of wax paper, coat sides of cake with the cake crumbs.

Let cake stand at room temperature for 20 minutes before serving.

As you can see, Pat was late for a reason. It took her hours, perhaps days, to get this cake done. It was delicious.

Having said that, this is a cake that probably no one will make. If anyone does, please send me a picture!! This cake is picture worthy. I made it once. I did not take a picture. Since the recipe was published in 1990, pictures were not yet digital and if I do have a picture, it is buried somewhere, I know not where.

Having shared a hard recipe with nectarines, let me make you happy and share an easy recipe for a nectarine blueberry crisp.

Nectarine Blueberry Crisp

TOPPING

- ¾ c. flour
- ⅓ lightly packed light brown sugar
- ⅓ sugar
- ¼ tsp. salt
- ¼ tsp. ground cinnamon
- ⅛ tsp. ground ginger
- 6 tbps. cold unsalted butter

FRUIT FILLING

- 1 ½ lbs. firm ripe nectarines
- 1 pt. blueberries (frozen are fine but take them out of the freezer early)
- ¼ c. sugar
- 2 Tbsp. flour

DIRECTIONS:

Preheat oven to 400.

To prepare the topping; Mix the flour, sugars, salt and spices in a medium mixing bowl (I just use the Cuisinart.) Cut in the butter until mixture resembles coarse meal. (I just pulse the machine).

To prepare the fruit filling: Pit the nectarines and cut into ⅓ inch thick slices. Toss the nectarines in a bowl with the blueberries, sugar, and flour. Pour the fruit into a 9 or 10-in. square baking dish, pyrex pie plate or individual tartlet pans. Sprinkle the topping evenly over the fruit.

Bake for 25-30 minutes or until the top is browned and the juices are bubbling up around the edge. Remove from the oven and cool for at least 15 minutes before serving.

Vanilla ice cream or whipped cream is a nice way to dress it up!!

NOTE:

If fruit is really juicy, a tad more flour in the fruit might be in order. Conversely... cut back on the granulated sugar when the fruit is sweet. It gets too sweet otherwise.

You could substitute strawberry and rhubarb (up the sugar to ½ c.), peach and blackberry/raspberry, apple and cranberry, pear (add ¼ c. slivered almonds in the topping).

This is a fabulous recipe and is adapted from Bradley Ogden, a famous chef. As an aside, we went to his restaurant in Larkspur for my retirement dinner. Pat was there. She wasn't late!!

O is for Onions

Life would not be worth living without onions.

And yet, as a kid I would not eat onions. Be they green, red, white, or yellow. Onion was not going to be on my plate, in my burger. No way. Which is another way of saying that we all grow up and open our minds to the onion. Well, most of us.

They are a cook's life's blood. Essential, no matter the color.

A hamburger without an onion is, well, don't bother. If you don't like them raw, you can sauté them because when they are sautéed, they become sweet. Surely, you can handle them then.

What would any spaghetti sauce be without onion? Less interesting. How about catsup? Same, same.

Onions are known to make grown men cry. Rayman has been known to don swimming goggles to shield his eyes from the chemical that is emitted from the onion when sliced. See picture below.

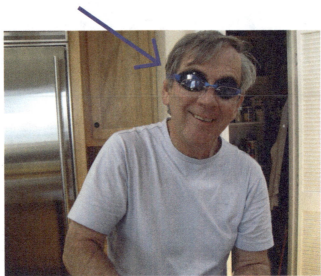

Not all onions offend like that. Spanish onions, Walla Wallas, onions from Hawaii. Maui Wowies? They can be quite sweet and/or mild. Red onions, also known as Bermudas, are great in salads. If they are strong, just soak them in cold water or hot water before using them raw. It cuts the acid and and tones them down.

I'll be the first to admit that they are no fun to chop or dice. Slicing isn't as bad. But, in the end, it is worth it.

Because onions are so ubiquitous, I am providing only one recipe for this tome.

Onion Panade

This recipe opens: "Cook the onions, lightly salted, in the butter over a very low heat, stirring occasionally, for about 1 hour, keeping them covered for the first 40 minutes."

As Russ Parsons, a writer for the L.A. Times said years ago, the instruction teaches us a lesson. First, salt those onions at the beginning. It will help them wilt faster and you want those onions wilted. And trap the heat while they brown. So easy, so elemental.

INGREDIENTS:

- 4 large onions, thinly sliced (about 1 ½ lb. or 6 cups)
- Salt
- ¼ c. butter
- ½ lb. dried bread, thinly sliced (about ⅓ inch)
- 6 ounces (3 cups) freshly grated Parmesan and Gruyere. I will leave it to you as to how much of each.
- Salted boiling water (about 4 cups)
- Cognac

Pair with 2021 Dresser Winery Petite Cab

DIRECTIONS:

Cook the onions, lightly salted, in one-fourth cup butter over a very low heat, stirring occasionally, for about 1 hour, keeping them covered for the first 40 minutes. If the heat is low enough and the saucepan of a heavy material, there will be no problem of coloration -- they should begin to caramelize lightly toward the end of an hour's time, at which point the flame may be turned up slightly and they should be stirred regularly until the entire mass is of a uniformly rich caramel color. Should there be signs of coloration too soon, the flame should be lowered even more, or the heat may be dispersed by separating the pan from the flame with a heat diffuser.

Spread slices of bread thickly with the onions, arrange a layer in the bottom of the casserole, sprinkle over a thick layer of cheese, and repeat the process, packing each layer gently and arranging the bread slices to avoid empty spaces. The last layer should be sprinkled only with cheese, and the casserole should not be more than two-thirds full at this point.

Bring the salted water to a boil in the same pan in which the onions were cooked. When it comes to a boil, pour it slowly and very carefully, at one single point against the side of the casserole, permitting the bread to swell and the mass to rise about 1 inch, or until obviously just floating, but no more (If you fear an unsteady hand, carefully ease the tip of a funnel down the side of the casserole to the bottom and pour the boiling water into the funnel.)

Cook on top of the stove, uncovered, over a very low heat, the surface maintaining a light, slow bubble for one-half hour. Add, as before, just enough boiling water to be certain that the body of the bread is submerged, sprinkle a bit more cheese over the surface. Sprinkle over a teaspoon of Cognac now, if you like, shave about 1 Tbsp. butter in paper-thin sheets from a firm cold block of butter, distributing them over the surface and transfer the casserole to a medium oven (325 to 350 degrees) for 1 hour, raising or lowering the temperature, if necessary, after about 40 minutes, depending on how the gratin is developing. The soup should be covered with a richly colored crust of gratin and should be served with a large spoon onto preheated plates.

A note from me. Warm your plates.

You can soak them in hot water, you can rinse them and put them in the microwave, or you can heat them in the oven, the toaster oven, the warming oven. It makes a lovely difference. I confess that I don't always do it. But when I don't, I wish I had.

I featured this recipe as recipe of the year, when I used to send out my favorite new recipe to my Xmas list people. That was fun while it lasted but I got very little feedback so abandoned the project when I went all digital.

This recipe is so yummy.

P is for Poetic Pasta

When I was young, about 13 years old, I had the responsibility of picking up my brother John, who was about 3 and enrolled in a pre-K program. Don't think it was called that. Think it was referred to as "nursery school." After picking him up, I'd walk him home and fix dinner. One of the things I liked to make was pasta. With a package of pasta, your world is set. Boil that salted water, throw that pasta in and when, according to the instructions on the package, time is up, fork a piece of pasta out of the pot, and throw it on the window. Someone told me that was how it was done. It may have been my mother. She was so not into cooking so it could have been her.

After scraping the pasta off the window, I would then taste it to see if it was done. Al dente was not a term I knew or used until I was much, much older. So, I'm not convinced I would have known if it was undercooked, overcooked or whatever. At such time when I deemed it done, there might be 10 pieces of pasta flung at the window which looked out on a common area. Anyone walking by would have gotten an eye full.

But, I digress.

Those were my first recollections of cooking pasta and I haven't stopped since. Pasta is, to me, a perfect food. Easy to make if you are so inclined (by make I mean, actually make the pasta.) Pasta is found on a grocery shelf in every market in America. Or in any market anywhere else in the world, for that matter.

Perhaps it is time for me to wax poetic. No funny stuff...just heartfelt feeling expressed in dramatic and artistic form for my dear readers.

One of the grand pleasures in life is knowing how to plate a great meal in minutes.

All muss and fuss set aside. A meal that can be orchestrated with minimum ingredients and yet be sublime. So, let me introduce to you... Sergeant Pepper's Lonely Hearts Club Band... no, no, no. That isn't right. But it might have been the genesis of dinner last night when pepper took a bold stand of being a major ingredient.

Pepper aka pepe is part of almost any dinner, but plays a secondary role, supporting actress if you will. Not so with this dish. No siree.

Let's first explore how it came to be that I decided on this particular dish. I was lazy. Walking 18 golf holes yesterday took its toll and so did the fact that I was stuck on said computer trying to correct a previous mistake I had made when I fell for a scam, gave out my credit card (luckily with the Portland address which is not my billing address) and had to call the bank to ask for a new card. Of course, this was the card that all our bills are paid by and with. We leave this card at home so we don't have to replace it if we lose it. No. I managed, still, with all that care, to screw up anyway.

Oops. I forgot. I'm am to wax poetic.

Okay. Back to my dinner which we all know can either be fabulous or what's the opposite of fabulous? A debacle? Unforced error?

Drum roll please. Cacio and Pepe. OMG...the king of the pasta world in simplicity and calories perhaps, though I doubt it. Alfredo is bound to have more calories. Essentially, you lovingly draw the water which in my case took about 3 minutes because we have a faulty thingie on our long necked goose. I mean long necked kitchen faucet that has hardly been used and the water is somehow constricted. But time is a beautiful thing and this allowed me to saunter around the kitchen with gin and tonic in hard and grind the pepper...the fresh ground scent perfuming the air with every twist. (As a practical matter, this also allowed me to exercise my right hand wrist as I waited for the pot to fill.

The water was then salted with a flourish which I first observed at an Italian opera, and the lid placed on the pot to hasten the boiling of the water. Another pan was enlisted in the effort and into it I gently, but lovingly, placed two tablespoons of butter which melted so slowly, you could visually imagine the molecules dancing in the pan. The pepper was placed with great care into the warm butter and the two did a waltz of such beauty that it brought tears to my eyes. That resulted in a luxurious butter/pepper sauce.

At last, the bubbles did their dance, and the pot was filled with dancing bubbles. Boiling is another way to describe it.

Once the pasta was tingling with excitement, I timed it for seven minutes and when the melodic tune of the timer went off, it was time to drain the spaghetti, leaving in reserve 1/2 cup of pasta water to gently place into the butter/pepper pan so the pasta could continue to cook. Into this, I accidentally spilled some water, but this, we will not dwell upon.

Another bit of beautiful butter was added to the glistening pan, then the cheeses. Both Reggiano and Romano were slowly added to the pasta and the pasta was tossed with tongs in such a way so that the cheese didn't, well, glob up (not a poetic word). OMG.

With a robust glass of red wine, dinner was plated and presented. Amen.

Cacio and Pepe

INGREDIENTS:

- Kosher salt
- 6 oz. pasta (such as egg tagliolini, bucatini, or spaghetti)
- 3 Tbsp. unsalted butter, cubed, divided
- 1 tsp. freshly cracked black pepper or more if you love pepper
- ¾ c. finely grated Grana Padano or Parmesan
- ⅓ c. finely grated Pecorino

Pair with 2021 Dresser Winery Good Times

DIRECTIONS:

1 Bring 3 quarts water to a boil in a 5-qt. pot. Season with salt; add pasta and cook, stirring occasionally, until about 2 minutes before tender. Drain, reserving ¾ cup pasta cooking water.

2 Meanwhile, melt 2 Tbsp. butter in a large heavy skillet over medium heat. Add pepper and cook, swirling pan, until toasted, about 1 minute.

3 Add ½ cup reserved pasta water to skillet and bring to a simmer. Add pasta and remaining butter. Reduce heat to low and add Grana Padano or Parmigiano Reggiano, stirring and tossing with tongs until melted. Remove pan from heat; add Pecorino, stirring and tossing until cheese melts, sauce coats the pasta, and pasta is al dente. (Add more pasta water if sauce seems dry.) Transfer pasta to warm bowls and serve.

Voila.

Now, let me admonish you not to substitute an inferior cheese. It's the main ingredient. Same with the pepper. It must be fresh ground. Don't bother to make this dish if you don't use the very best ingredients. It will not be as good.

Q is for Quail

QUAIL LEGS COURTESY OF
POETRY HUNTING CLUB

Have you ever attended a "Just Say No" seminar? That's where a timeshare outfit sends you an invitation to a sales pitch where they give you the fabulous opportunity to spend thousands of dollars on a vacation deal. You give them cash up front and you get in return, a week or two of vacation time at a resort. We know many of our friends have gone to these seminars because they are now proud owners of vacation time. Well, having worked in the world of finance, we have never been able to pencil out one of these offers— where it made any financial sense to us— and so we dubbed these sales pitches the "Just Say NO' seminars.

There are certain perks to these sale pitches which pique our interest... mainly, the free golf that comes with the deal or, say, a $100 to spend on dinner at the restaurant. So, that's how we ended up at a restaurant with 4 of our crazy friends in Carmel Highlands early in this century.

The Highlands Inn is very much a high-end kind of place. The location is exquisite, in that it is precariously perched on jagged rocks above the rollicking Pacific Ocean and for that you pay a pretty price. There are probably hundreds of thousands of people who have never seen the U.S. Pacific Ocean. They are landlocked in, say, Iowa and the don't really get how beautiful this place is. They can see it in the pictures or on TV and that's great. But to hear the sounds, experience the fog rolling in, to see the seals on the rocks... well, they will not be able to really understand how special this area of California is. But that was where we were. And it was time for dinner.

So, after a warm up round of cocktails in the room our friends', Tom and Ruthie, we carefully walked down the hill in the rain (This was February and the rainy season.) and that is where we entered the on-property restaurant. When you enter this very special space, you step down into the tiered dining room which is encapsulated in floor to ceiling glass. Dramatic and stunning, really. You see, Tom and Ruthie had received a $100 dining credit, and they generously proposed to share it with us, the other four. Additionally, Ruthie, had called ahead and negotiated with the staff a deal that if we bought one bottle of their wine they would waive the corkage fee on the bottle we were bringing with us. Ruthie thinks of everything. No stone is left unturned if Ruthie has anything to say about it. We were thrilled with her generosity as well as her fast thinking because their corkage fee was around $25/bottle.

Why do we put up with corkage fees? Oh, I know. People collect and age wine and when they go out to dinner they like to bring their wine along so they can enjoy it with the meal. Restaurants know this and they, to my way of thinking, take advantage of winers (people with their own bottles). The theory is that the fee may keep people from bringing their own bottle (BYOB!!) and therefore buying what the restaurant offers. This is in direct conflict with what winers want, don't you think? So, you take your wine that you bought for, say, $30 and you are required to pay anywhere from $10-$40 to have someone stand at the table and uncork or unscrew the bottle for you. So, you do the math and you figure out that your $30 bottle of wine just cost you $45 or more before the first sip. It just doesn't feel good. But I must move on here.

While being seated in the restaurant, one would not have been able to ignore the real furs in the room. Shoulders were draped. Diamonds of the 8 karat variety were on display on the fingers of well-coiffed ladies. Oh, the silk shirts of the men in attendance looked elegant with the ties they wore. And then, there was us. We looked nice but nothing fancy. Call it country club casual. Oh, well. That was okay. We are who we are. I yam what I yam. (Perhaps I will do Y is for Yams...a possibility).

But I digress. The menus were presented. OMG. $15 for salad. $20 for soup. $50 for an entree. OMG. The $100 credit was about enough to cover an appetizer which I immediately ruled out as being too expensive. Looks were exchanged. Our friend Arnie grew red in the face. Well. What could be done? We couldn't get up and leave. The name of the game moved from awe of setting to shock of price. We would figure it out. So, when the waiter came to take our order, Arnie, a man with a barrel chest planted on an almost 6- foot frame, ordered the quail. The waiter, in tuxedo, said, "Yes? And for your entree?" Arnie replied, "That is my entree." The waiter bent down a bit closer to Arnie and explained in a very low voice, "That is a small portion, sir." Arnie was resolute. "That's fine. Quail is my order." The rest of us ordered, and as I recall, the others ordered entrees. No salad. No soup. No appetizers. Just entrees.

The other thing was the wine. When the waiter brought the wine lists, he schlepped out two enormous books. One for red and one for white. OMG. The least expensive bottle was a white wine for $40. Believe me when I tell you that a person could spend thousands on a bottle of wine. Our party settled for a bottle of white for $40. We are retired after all. So... this is how the one percenters live. Who knew?

There does seem to be a relationship with the price of the food in an establishment and the size of the plate. The more it costs, the bigger the plate. Now, psychologically, I'm not entirely convinced that this is a good thing, and I use this experience as a perfect example of what I mean. The waiters approached the table. The dishes were enormous so it took several waiters. And, there it was. The QUAIL. Only it was not the whole quail. It wasn't half a quail. It was a quail leg. It was about the size of your pinky and it was artfully displayed on a plate about 14 x 14 inches. OMG. Well, this is about the time that the snorting started. Everyone (except Arnie) started laughing. The thing is that when you are really, really laughing and trying to suppress it because of all the fur and diamonds around you, the peels of laughter emerge as snorts. And once you start snorting... well, let's put it this way... you can't snort just once. It is followed by more snorts. OMG.

And then there is the question of how a big man eats a tiny quail leg. Just let your imagination run away with you. It was quite a sight. And then, when he had finished his quail leg, he had to fill his time, and he did this by watching the rest of us eat our ENTREES. While doing this, he leans over to me (I'm seated to his right), and whispered... "I only paid $9.99 for the wine I brought." I was horror struck. Surely the waiter must have known. OH, how embarrassing.... but not quite as embarrassing as my snorting!!

Did other people notice? The ENTIRE restaurant noticed. We were the riff-raff... who let us in? Glances were stolen. Looks were exchanged. Heads were nodded. But really, we had more fun than everyone. It was a total hoot. And because of it, quail will always hold a special place in my memory. You can't make this stuff up.

R is for Rice

Every cook needs to know how to cook rice. Having said that, I have ruined more than one pan when attempting to cook rice. And I have a sneaky suspicion that I am not alone.

And who hasn't hummed the ditty, "Rice a Roni, A San Francisco Treat" to themselves over the years? Such a catchy tune.

One of my favorite recipes with rice is paella. A Spanish dish that is great for a party. It feeds many at the same time. And it shines. So, now that we have a Spaniard in our extended family, I must pay homage to this versatile dish. My only regret is that I do not have a pit in the back yard. However, life goes on. Historically, paella was cooked in the fields over an open fire and while I would love to replicate it, it aint' going to happen exactly that way.

There are a variety of paella recipes, but generally they call for Bomba rice. Bomba rice absorbs much more liquid than other rice, and yet it doesn't get soggy. Arborio rice is often substituted for those that balk at the price tag of Bomba. As they say, pick your poison.

My philosophy of cooking is like my philosophy concerning covid shots. Trust the experts. Experts know what they are talking about. I do try to seek out good advice on cooking which has lead to having a library of cookbooks, many of which I have donated to our local library. With seemingly every recipe on earth available through the google machine, I've let some of them go. Lots of them. Hundreds, perhaps. I was addicted to cookbooks. Still, have a hard time not buying them. But the internet has curbed my appetite, if you will pardon the pun.

According to someone who looked into paella, "rice loaded up with shrimp, squid, sausage, chicken, peas, pimientos, and maybe hunks of fish—wasn't really paella at all. The original paella was valenciana. Valencians agree, paella was a dish not of the seaside but of the huertas: saffron-flavored rice combined with rabbit and chicken, three kinds of beans, and snails in the shell. Seafood paella was a later invention and, according to Valencians, is never made with meat or fowl." This info is per Bruce Schoenfeld in an article in Saveur from the early oughts.

My takeaway is that fish and chicken and rabbit are the most likely candidates for a good paella. And sometimes less is more as far as the ingredients. Interestedly, beans are included in paellas too.

So, rather than highlight a particular recipe, I'd say find your own, try to cook it over an open fire in a barbecue device, and enjoy the heck out of it. Oh, and be sure to add saffron if you want to get close to the real deal.

Oh, and one last bit of advice. Make the required sofrito. Paellas start with a sofrito, of chopped vegetables cooked in oil—typically garlic and tomatoes, and sometimes onions and Spanish red peppers called ñoras. The longer the sofrito cooks, the darker and more intensely flavored the paella will be. And, I have read that once you've stirred the rice with the cooked sofrito and the stock, just leave it alone, uncovered. When the rice is cooked through, after 20 minutes or so, feel free to turn up the heat to create a flavorful crust called socarrat on the bottom of the pan. We start cooking it on the stove, and when all the fish, for instance, have been added, we take it out to the Weber barbecue and set it on the grate. Under the grate is a fire burned down with a few chunks of soaked wood added to create smoke. Left uncovered to cook, the dish picks up the smoke flavor. An added bonus.

Which brings me to my saffron story.

The Morrows invited us over for a super supper which we cooked together. One of the dishes was one that required saffron. Now, Greg and Teri, being who they are, were very kind to pre-measure and prep many things ahead of time. When the recipe said to add the saffron, I opened up the container and in went the saffron. Much to the horror of our hosts, it was not pre-measured. I was only to put a bit in. But, but.

OMG. I really screwed up. So, when I returned home, I sent them a thank you gift of saffron. Lots and lots of saffron. I felt better. Now I giggle at the whole saffron affair.

One other transgression!!

One of my blogs from Spain seems appropriate here:

" Well, today is our last Thursday in Spain. And for the occasion, Rayman and I planned to cook dinner for the group.

MENU DE DAY
- Roast organic chicken stuffed with lemon
- Bread Salad
- Roasted potatoes and garlic cloves cooked in olive oil and butter
- Fresh boiled asparagus
- Ice cream
- Vino

And what was really interesting is that we planned to do all the cooking on the wood stove in the kitchen. So, Rayman gathered the pre-cut wood, the matches and some paper. A fire was started. Successfully. You could smell it in the house. I brought the chicken to room temperature for even cooking, Current thinking is that bringing food to room temp is passe so do what you like. There were two chickens as there were 6 of us and the chickens were small to our way of thinking. The bread salad involved plumping the raisins (The recipe called for currants but we were lucky to find raisins). Toasting the pine nuts. Slicing a spring onion. Washing the frisee. Sauting the onion and garlic.

The potatoes were cut up and slathered in olive oil and a few teaspoons of butter just to gild the lily. Oh, and unpeeled cloves of garlic were tossed in.

The owner of the house told us the fire would take about an hour's lead time. So we did that, lighting it about 3:30. And then we popped the potatoes and chickens into the oven at 4:30. I kept saying, "Rayman, I don't smell the chicken." He would go to the stove and check the fire. Yep, the fire was burning. The top of stove was hot, hot, hot. Well, then. They must be cooking. This conversation was repeated about three times. "Rayman, I don't smell the chicken cooking." Rayman replied, "Maybe we can't smell it because it is well sealed." "Rayman, I still can't smell the chicken." The reply was, "Well, it must be cooking. That fire is raging."

We didn't want to open the door, because the temp dropped 50 degrees (at least) when we put the stuff into the oven. Well. Finally, we decided we had better check. The chicken and potatoes had been in about an hour. They weren't stone cold. But they sure as heck weren't cooked. So, Terry, the engineer by training, came in and he and Rayman discussed possibilities. I found the owner's phone number and called him. The conversation was not going well, what with his Spanish and my English. I implored Janis to speak with him. She did. Then we got somewhere. The fire had been started in the right place. There were two possibilities. So, Rayman decided to crank the heat up. He fed the furnace 3 pine cones, and 3 more logs. Voila. The chicken started to make sounds, crackling sounds. We were on our way.

We let the food cook about an hour more. When I took it out, meat was falling off the drumstick bone.

But I digress.

I baked the bread part of the bread salad while the chickens rested. The asparagus was cooked on top of the wood stove. We kept things warm by having them just on or near the top of the stove. And it all came together. A minor miracle since none of us had any experience in wood stove cooking.

No matter which way it went, this was going to be the blog material. We had a 50-50 chance. Oh, and we sat down to the table at 7:30 or so. Gives new meaning to the idea of slow food.

The other thing that happened was we as a group had not been out for a meal together all week. It was on the radar that we would do so tomorrow. So instead of playing Parchese, scrabble, bridge or some other game, the Packers and the Bucks researched restaurants in the area on their electronic devices. I was all wrapped up in mine too because I was trying to figure out how to post a darn video on my blog. Without success. So, there was much conversation about many things. And, we all concluded that it is very difficult to eat in Spain unless you eat tapas early or eat dinner late. Not much in between. Websites were consulted, TripAdvisor was asked. At one point, Dorothy found that someone from Santa Maria, CA had visited and critiqued one of the restaurants right down the street. "Can you imagine?", she said. Then she read the glowing comments. Terry said, "Well, just remember, they are from Santa Maria." I think the way it was resolved is that calls would be made in the morning to ascertain if
1. Was the restaurant open on Fridays ?
2. Did they serve lunch at lunch time?
3. Was lunch more than tapas?
4. What hours did they serve lunch?
5. What was on the menu? This with language differences.

What could possibly go wrong?

In the event that things did go wrong, there was plenty of leftover chicken, some leftover bread salad, some leftover asparagus, two chicken carcasses, and a myriad of other things we had to throw away since we were leaving on Saturday. Just saying.

We muddled through. "

Another great rice dish is jambalaya from Louisiana. I attribute it to Louisiana because that is where I first ate it. At Paul Prudhomme's restaurant in New Orleans. It was powerful and delicious.

Here is my rendition of his

Poorman's Jambalaya.

INGREDIENTS:

- 4 small bay leaves
- 1 tsp. salt
- 1 tsp. white pepper
- 1 tsp. dry mustard
- 1 tsp. ground red pepper (preferably cayenne). Beware if you don't like hot.
- 1 tsp. gumbo file (file powder) (optional) and good luck finding it.
- 1/2 tsp. ground cumin
- 1/2 tsp. black pepper
- 1/2 tsp. dried thyme leaves
- 4 Tbsp. butter
- 6 ounces tasso (about 1 1/2 cups) OR 6 ounces other smoked ham, diced. I like Cure 81... less heat, great flavor.
- 6 ounces smoked andouille sausages (about 1 heaping cup) OR 6 ounces kielbasa, diced. Don't use that much andouille unless you live near a fire department.
- 1 1/2 c. onions, chopped
- 1 1/2 c. celery, chopped
- 1 c. bell pepper, chopped
- 1 1/2 tsp. minced garlic
- 2 c. uncooked rice (preferably converted)
- 4 c. of chicken stock (if not salt-free, adjust salt)

Pair with 2021 Dresser Winery Cabernet Sauvignon

DIRECTIONS:

Seasoning Mix: Combine the first 9 ingredients in a small bowl and set aside.

Jambalaya: Use a large, heavy skillet, cast iron is best; over high heat melt butter; add tasso or whatever you choose to use and andouille, or ham and sausage, and cook 5 minutes, stirring occasionally.

Add onions, celery, bell pepper, seasoning mix and garlic; stir and cook 10-12 minutes until well browned, scraping the bottom of the pan well.

Stir in rice and cook 5 minutes, again scraping the pan bottom often; add stock.

Bring mixture to boil; reduce heat and simmer, uncovered, about 20 minutes, until rice is tender but still a bit crunchy; stir a bit toward the end of the cooking time; remove bay leaves and serve.

Note: you can use other rice. It is reported that converted has more nutrients. Who knows? I have always used converted because Paul said to use it.

S is for Skeet

We belonged to a gourmet dinner group. The group had been in existence for years and it all started when our good friend, JoEllen, decided to take matters into her own hands and organize. Somehow, we knew people who knew people; and so her people called our people and that is how we were invited to join the group.

At this point ,you may be wondering about gourmet groups in general. After years of accumulated experience, I've put together a small tutorial that may or may not come in handy for you, the dear reader, in which I will characterize the "Pitfalls" to avoid.

1. Invitees

Only invite people into the group who know how to cook. You should be careful about this as there are people out there who think they know how to cook. But you have to do research. Is their definition of cooking opening up an appetizer they bought in the freezer section of Trader Joe's? If so, you may want to pass on that prospect. Do they think a floating island is actually, well, a floating island? May want to pass on that one. Do they buy canned peas? Really? For the life of me, I cannot figure out why peas are canned anymore. Have you looked at the canned food section of your local market? It is the mystery spot of the grocery store. Okay, I like canned tomatoes. And canned tomato paste. And canned tomato sauce. But canned peas? Canned yams? Canned asparagus? Why would anyone buy these things?

Invite only people who drink wine and/or beer. There is the occasional exception to that rule, like my cousin, Sue. But in general, you should be looking for people who like to have fun, good food and enjoy wine. Avoid at all costs the person who doesn't "hold their liquor." You know what I mean. If they have too much to drink and end up under the dining room table singing, say, "Light My Fire," this may cause some problems. Also, there are generally two types of people in this world. Uppers and downers. Only invite uppers. One downer can ruin an entire group. Really. This is a universal truth. You know the type. Everything is either a problem that must be bitched about (And yes, men bitch too.) Or they are unhappy about just about everything. And people who complain about their spouses should not be invited under any circumstances. "He always watches TV and never pays any attention to me. I give him ideas and he won't ever agree" might be the type of speaker you want to avoid, because this will probably turn into a reoccurring theme over the years with more or less distain, and it will get old. No one will enjoy hearing the complaints about a spouse. If it's that bad, leave, for goodness sakes.

That reminds me of a story I like to repeat on occasion. We were invited to a country club golf tourney, and we accepted the invitation. The format was one that turned a 5 hour game into a six hour game which is entirely too long for a golf game. So, there we were. And we were paired with another couple who had played in this tournament since, perhaps, the beginning of time. So, I let it be known that the game was too slow. That is when the other man explained that this is how it is. It had always been this way and, by George, it was that way again. This did not deter me. I mentioned it again. Again, he told me how the cow ate the cabbage. Finally, he had had enough. When I continued to carry on about this, he looked at me and said, "Look. This tournament is always slow so you might as well stop complaining about it so we can all have fun." And you know what? He was right. And I thanked him on the next hole after I had time to stop being embarrassed. Actually, he did me a huge favor which I will always be thankful for...because it has applicability to almost anything and everything. Well adjusted people don't like complainers. And hearing the same complaint over and over is a real downer. So...all that to say that you should avoid downers.

Okay. So no downers and no faux cooks. Find people who love good food and wine.

2. Organization

Over the years, I've belonged to many groups. One type of group is one in which the host cooks everything. There are a few pitfalls with this format which the reader should be aware of. This is entirely too hard. Not only do you have to cook the entire meal, the house must be clean. Too much work. Too hard. Too expensive. Forgetaboutit. The other problem is that invariably when it comes time for the final couple to do the dinner, they will suddenly quit the group. Family emergency perhaps. Yes, the emergency will be that they don't want to or can't do it. You think I jest? Uh uh. This has happened to me twice, and the only reason it didn't happen three times is that I never joined another one of those groups which was formatted that way. And my recommendation is that you do not get involved with that type of format. It will break your heart.

The best way to set up a group is to use the "potluck" method. By this I mean, the hostess sets the menu or theme. Let's say you are hosting and you want to do a Croatian theme. Just kidding. Say a New Orleans theme. You can either assign the subtending dishes to the other cooks or you can ask for volunteers, as in, let the people decide. And, you can assign the actual recipe or not. So, Mary Jane brings a specific type of salad, say Waldorf using your recipe, or she volunteers for salad and brings her own creation. I know of one group where the woman was a control freak. Incidentally, the cook could be a man. It is just in this case, the cook was a woman.

Okay. So she liked to control everything and this manifested itself in her assigning each recipe. Really, the only thing was that the other cooks hated her choices (too expensive, too hard, too too). This did nothing to promote espirit de corps. And the lady may have in the end nurtured her reputation as a control freak. So, I say, avoid this way of organizing. It may not lead to success. Instead, have the host/hostess decide the theme. Share the theme with the group. Ask for volunteers for whatever you need. Assign based on first-come, first-serve. And let it fly.

The other thing is the wine. Ask each couple to bring a bottle. Some groups have each person bring a bottle. That is okay except for drinking and driving. Whatever. The only real problem with the wine is that some people bring a $2.99/bottle champagne and others share a $40 bottle. Rules may be instituted to mitigate this problem. Just depends. Just be aware of this sticking point. For one holiday dinner we hosted, we asked that the wine be at least a $20/bottle. Really didn't want to drink Gallo jug wine with the prime rib. This solved that problem.

3. Decide on a Number

How many to have in the group? Six? Eight? Twenty four? Again. Depends. Our friend, JoEllen, organized the most successful group I've ever belonged to. She invited 12 couples into the group. Then she came up with a schedule whereby every other month 3 couples individually hosted a dinner for 8 (6 plus the host/hostess).

Well. This is a nightmare for the person running the group unless they are really into it and enjoy this activity. JoEllen loved doing the schedule, and she was good at it. I tried my hand at it and it made me mentally unbalanced. Things can pop up. Like, you hear complaints from the peanut gallery. "I haven't been to their house." "I hosted more than the Wongs." You can imagine. So...unless you enjoy doing schedules, I have concluded the best way of organizing such a group is to draw for names.

Throw a party where everyone comes and brings an appetizer. Liquor up the crowd and then draw names. The host couples draw according to the schedule of hosts which should be pre-determined so that no one has to "over host", or "under host". Also the host selection should be shaken up because if the same hosts host at the same time (Feb/Mar and then again Apr/May), flexibility is greatly inhibited. Because the schedule is mostly by chance, no one can complain about a darn thing. Well, they can. But it would fall on deaf ears. In my case, it did. All you have to do is write down the names and publish the schedule.

Along with the schedule, a list of rules is a good idea as well as a list of members, their phone numbers, email addresses, home address, and a list of things people don't like to eat or are allergic to.

Example:

The goals for the group are to have a fun event and enjoy a variety of food and wine. We've set up some general guidelines, and we want to emphasize flexibility within those guidelines. Much discretion is given to the hosting couples.

So, enjoy!! Bon Appetit

> Requests we have of you!!
>
> Dinners, lunches or brunches are scheduled every two months. The hosting couple will coordinate the date and time within the two month period.
>
> When you are the hosting couple, please contact the other couples in your group early in the 2-month period, hopefully no later than the first week of the period.
>
> If you're on a special diet which will influence what you'll eat, please let the hosting couple know.
>
> The schedule for the 2023-2024 follows on the next two pages. Also included is the list of the group members, their contact information as well as the likes/dislikes info.
>
> Bon Appetit

And that's about it.

But, I digress. This was a chapter with the name of S is for Skeet. So we really need to get back to the subject.

My Mom with doves, circa 1935 on Vine Street in Paso Robles, CA

The very same person who organized the most successful group I've known is also an avid collector of Junior League cookbooks. Her laundry room is not your typical laundry room. Yes, this is still on that subject. You could have a dance in her laundry room, but JoEllen decided that instead of a dance floor she would use the extra space to store her library (literally) of cookbooks. The other thing you need to know about JoEllen is that I'm quite sure she has never repeated a dish ever...that is, she cooks a recipe from a cookbook once and then she never does it again. This is actually a very good idea because then the cook does not have to remember where in the heck that recipe for tangerine aspic is located. But the other thing is you need to have a lot of cookbooks to pull that off... remember, that habit was formed before the internet and apps and all that stuff that we use today.

Well, JoEllen was driving one day in a rural area and saw a sign for "Skeet Shoot Today." And so that got her to wondering what type of animal a skeet was, and if she shot and killed one, how would she cook it. She thought she must have a recipe for it. So, she went home and looked through all her cookbooks and could not find a recipe. And that's when she asked her husband if he knew how to cook a skeet.

The rest is history. Except that she still threatens to write a cookbook called *How to Cook a Skeet*. I am completely supportive of this idea. Fricassee of Skeet. Barbecued Skeet. Boiled Skeet. The possibilities are endless.

Fricassee of clay pigeon just doesn't have the same ring.

This info can be filed under the heading that you learn something new every day.

Note: skeet is a verb. It's the clay pigeon that I visualized as a skeet. The proper thing to cook would be a clay pigeon. And in the latest news, there is a guy named Clay Pigeon... yep, found him on the internet. He is a DJ somewhere. Well, that takes the cake.

T is for Tomato

Look at that tomato? Is the speaker referring to a sexy woman or a vegetable or a fruit?
Well, they could be talking about a sexy woman or a fruit. But not a veggie. And tomato, the Spanish one, means "fat thing." An apt description. However, did you know that a tomatillo is also a tomato, a Mexican tomato? And the Greek scientific name translates to wolf peach?

As a true fruit, it develops from the ovary of the plant after fertilization, its flesh comprising the pericarp walls. The fruit contains hollow spaces full of seeds and moisture, called locular cavities. These vary, among cultivated species, according to type. Some smaller varieties have two cavities, globe-shaped varieties typically have three to five, beefsteak tomatoes have a great number of smaller cavities, while paste tomatoes have very few, very small cavities.

That may be TMI but I found it interesting.

Tomatoes are an abused fruit. Agribusiness has turned them from a delicious item to something akin to cardboard. Do not buy these tomatoes. A dish is only as good as its ingredients. In Portland, there is a bakery called Grand Central, and in the summer, at the height of fruit season, they make a BLT to die for and it's all about the tomatoes. Once the tomatoes start waning, the fruit is not good so the bakery stops making them. And that is how we all might want to live our lives.

When it is **not** tomato season, I use canned tomatoes. There are many good varieties including the Muir Glen fire-roasted tomatoes. And, if I'm hankering for a fresh tomato, I only buy the cherry tomatoes. They will pass muster most of the time.

Tomatoes are in salads, in salsas, in stir fries, in tarts, in egg dishes… and the list goes on. Here I present an excellent recipe that you will love.

Shakshouka.

A Middle Eastern delight.

INGREDIENTS:

- 3 Tbsp. olive oil
- 1 large onion, halved and thinly sliced
- 1 large red bell pepper, seeded and thinly sliced
- 3 garlic cloves, thinly sliced
- 1 tsp. ground cumin
- 1 tsp. sweet paprika
- ⅛ tsp. ground cayenne, or to taste
- 1 (28-ounce) can whole plum tomatoes with their juices, coarsely chopped. I buy the tomatoes crushed. Saves a step.
- ¾ tsp. kosher salt, plus more as needed
- ¼ tsp. black pepper, plus more as needed
- 5 ounces feta, crumbled (about 1 ¼ cups)
- 6 large eggs
- Chopped cilantro, for serving. Allergic? Substitute parsley or basil.
- Hot sauce, for serving

Pair with 2021 Dresser Winery Petite Sirah

DIRECTIONS:

Heat oven to 375 degrees. Heat oil in a large skillet suitable for tomatoes over medium-low. Add onion and bell pepper. Cook gently until very soft, about 20 minutes. Add garlic and cook until tender, 1 to 2 minutes; stir in cumin, paprika and cayenne and cook 1 minute. Pour in tomatoes and season with ¾ tsp. salt and ¼ tsp. pepper; simmer until tomatoes have thickened, about 10 minutes. Taste and add more salt and pepper if needed. Stir in crumbled feta.

Gently crack eggs into skillet over tomatoes. Season eggs with salt and pepper. Transfer skillet to oven and bake until eggs are just set, 7 to 10 minutes. Sprinkle with cilantro and serve with hot sauce.

If it is in the dead of summer, you can cook the entire thing on the stove top by just putting a lid on the pan until the eggs are cooked. Just check often. A runny egg is the target.

Tomatoes don't do well when cooked in certain pans. I recommend always using stainless steel because if cooked in a reactive pan, the tomato will take like something metallic. Not a good taste. And non stick pans should be avoided for the sake of the pan. The tomatoes are highly acidic and they break down the non-stick chemicals in the pan.

Another thing to be aware of are local tomato festivals.

Check out locations on a website. Here is one:

If you live in Ohio or some other exotic locale, google "Tomato festivals near me'" to find a festival.

When I was a kid, my grandfather always planted a garden that had tomatoes in it. I would just snatch one off the vine, and then eat it right then and there. Juice running down my chin, the tomato was warm as the summer day, and the smell was heavenly… That smell is the smell you should look for when and if sniffing of tomatoes (and other fruit and veggies) ever comes back into vogue. If you can't smell the tomato, don't buy it. Or buy one and take it home to check it out. If it is irresistible, go back immediately and buy more if you need them.

And cultivate friends that have tomato vines, because once one tomato ripens, they all seem to ripen, and it is then when you might score some homegrown fruit. Or grow your own if you are lucky enough to have the time, the space, the inclination and the climate.

 is for Utensils

> Hey diddle diddle
> The cat and the fiddle
> The cow jumped over the moon
> The little dog laughed to see such sport
> And the dish ran away with the spoon

Have you visited a kitchen store lately? it is absolutely amazing how many gadgets they sell. Who thinks this stuff up? And why do they think we need it. Hot dog cookers? Forman grills? A tool for every occasion or need.

If I bought all this stuff, where would I put it? And when I put it there, how would I find it? My kitchen would have to be the size of a Sur la Table store.

On the flip side, American ingenuity is impressive. Encounter a problem. Figure out a solution. Feel so passionate about it that it gets made, advertised and sold. Who knew they needed an avocado scoop? a pineapple peeler? an electric chocolate melter? It's pretty impressive...really.

So this got me to thinking about what utensils I absolutely could not live without, and the first thing that jumped into my head was knives. You cannot work in your kitchen without a knife. And your life becomes easier as you add a few more knives to the collection. Personally, I own about ten big knives and use about one of them regularly. It fits my hand. It's not too big or too small. All the other knives I could live without... except for the paring knife. I really use the paring knife a lot. Paring knives are great for jalapenos and serranos.... as well as other smaller jobs.

Knives should be kept sharp. This is something I fail to do. Rayman loves to get out the steel and scrape the knives across it just at the moment that I need something minced pronto. It never fails. That is my method for keeping my knives sharp. If all my knives are dull at the same time, I bring out my electric knife sharpener (a tool which fits into the American ingenuity category.) Then I do them all at once. A dull knife is a drag. So keep those knives sharp.

Sharp knives cut through everything including your fingers much better. One Thanksgiving I had sharp knives. I was busy chopping chard and talking to my guests at the same time and voila, I sliced my finger open. This necessitated a drive to the community hospital where I opted for a butterfly bandage rather than stitches. I still have the scar. So, be careful of those sharp knives and practice proper knife safety. If you aren't sure what that is, google it. I'm sure there is a YouTube demonstration on the proper way to handle a knife. Most folks don't know how to hold a knife properly.

The next thing I couldn't live without is a rubber scraper. Some people like me call them spatulas. However, many think of spatulas as those tools that help you flip pancakes. And these people are right. We're all right. Can't we just get along? Just kidding. Whatever you call the rubber scraper, I couldn't get by without one.

Have you ever been seated at restaurant bar where the food is being cooked? Ever noticed their pans? They do not use fancy pans. And the pans they use look abused. No All Clad this or copper that. But, they do use pans and plenty of them. For me, your average kitchen cook, my favorite pans are my copper pans and my cast iron pans. I have other name brand pans. All-Clad stainless, Calphalon sauce pans. These are fine, but I love my copper pans and my cast iron pans. Rather than getting hung up on brands, its important to have a variety of pans. And sizes and shapes. A 10 to 12 inch skillet is important. A pot, preferably stainless steel, for making sauces and boiling pasta, or making beans. A dutch oven. A few saucepans for smaller jobs. A double boiler. I use my double boiler all the time. Actually I have two and, of course, there is a story around that.

I burned one of my double boilers up one time. Put something on the stove and completely forgot about it until the bottom of my pan was so black and so crusty and so warped, that the pan was scarred for life. And this wasn't the first time. I'm hoping that I'm not the only person that has done this just because that would make me feel, well, inadequate. So, I needed a new bottom pan for my double boiler.

My small double boiler also went to pan heaven because I neglected it while it was on the stove. The problem was my small double boiler was an antique. A Farberware pan from the 60s. Finding a replacement proved to be impossible. I looked and I looked. No one makes a small double boiler anymore. And, I was just looking for the bottom unit. I kept the top unit hoping I could find a replacement. Well, years went by. Then one day I was behind my uncle's house cleaning up the yard, and there it was. A Farberware double boiler bottom unit. What? How did this land up here, I wondered. Well, my grandmother had the same pan that I did, and when she died, he must have kept it and then used it to feed stray cats in the neighborhood. My uncle loved cats. He had cats since he was in his 40's. His cats had all been house cats. But he also loved stray cats and had a habit of feeding them, and using my grandmother's every day dishes and pots and pans, apparently, to feed them.

So, I just picked up that pan, and have had it ever since. And I love it for melting chocolate which I do a lot for things like that chocolat mousse!!

I need a grater for cheese and carrots and stuff like that. Microplanes are all the rage now and I understand why. You cannot achieve the same result from a knife so this makes a grater indispensable. That is also true with a funnel. Every kitchen should have at least one funnel for, well, funneling liquids from one container to another.

An electric mixer. Everyone needs an electric mixer. Again, I have two. A handheld and a standard mixer. Many times I use both to achieve the results required in a recipe. The mousse comes to mind. If you don't bake, a mixer isn't nearly as important. And you can live without one...a whisk and a copper pan come to mind as do a bowl and a fork. But really people, the electric mixer makes life easy, and, if you have a standard mixer, you can get attachments for making pasta or making sausages. Required? No. Nice to have. Yes. And now you see how easy it is to slip off the reservation. A whisk here, a mixer there and pretty soon you end up with Sur la Table.

So, what else must I have? A strainer. Preferably several in different sizes. You can sift flour in them. Rinse blueberries in them. Rinse and sift. Two very important functions in cooking. And, maybe that's the way to approach this issue of utensils. What does cooking require of us? What functions do we perform while cooking?

Boiling. You need pans to boil. Frying. You need pans to fry. Braising. You need a pot/pan for that. Steaming. Double boiler for steaming. Chopping, slicing, mincing, dicing…hand me the knife, please. Rinsing. A strainer for that. Moving food from one container to the other. A spatula, a flipper. A spoon.

Well, I wouldn't want to be without a slotted spoon as well as a ladle. Both are very good tools for specific issues in the cooking department.

And a dish? Bowls must be involved in cooking. Lots of bowls if you have the room. If not, a nested set is ideal for easy storage and a variety of sizes wrapped into one neat package. The small little bowls that are used to pre-measure for your mise en place are highly recommended and take up little room.

Then there are the pie plates and cake pans. Pie plates are great for serving watermelon, dipping fish into batter and then crumbs, say. If you have to have just one size, make it a 9 incher. Cake pans can serve double duty too but I rarely use them that way. I generally just make cakes in them. Don't bake? Forget cake pans. If you do bake, 8 and 9 inches are a must. An angel food pan is a must. A springform is a must. Loaf pans, maybe. Muffins pans. Cupcake pans. Ramekins.

I've left things out, perhaps, but the above listed are the most important.

V is for Vinegar

It could have been veal. It would have been vegetables. But my favorite V is Vinegar.

The first memory of vinegar which I had was the smell of it when my grandmother would rinse my hair in it. Once applied, the vinegar made easy work of the snarls that graced my crown. My hair was very fine, very thick. Tangles would ensue. But never fear, vinegar was there. Can't say that I minded it.

Vinegar is a miracle worker in the kitchen. It brightens salads, it brightens stews. It cleans things. It is featured in rhyme such as Jack and Jill:

> Up Jack got
> And home did trot,
> As fast as he could caper;
> Went to bed
> To mend his head
> With vinegar and brown paper.

Vinegar and brown paper was actually used as a treatment for bruises. Maybe I'll try that.

The chemical formula for vinegar is CH_3COOH. Who knew? Probably the high school chemistry teacher I never knew because I was afraid to take chemistry. Silly me.

Cooking is chemistry when you get right down to it.

Baking soda, yeast, baking powder— all are chemicals used in baking. If you are a baker, you are essentially a chemist. And that is another good reason to pay attention to the writer of the recipe.

Last spring, I made a homemade batch of vinegar with a "mother" and red wine. Might try white wine vinegar this year. The process is easy, confusing, and time consuming, but don't let that stop you. It was gratifying when I gave some to a friend and they actually liked it. Being my virgin voyage on the boat of vinegar, I was unsure. But sure enough, it turned out just fine.

Chicken with Vinegar and Olives

(adapted from the NYTimes)

DIRECTIONS:

Heat oven to 450 degrees. Place chicken on a rimmed baking sheet that is lined with parchment paper and toss with turmeric and 2 Tbsp. olive oil, and season with salt and pepper. Make sure chicken is skin-side up, then pour vinegar over and around chicken and place in the oven.

Bake chicken, without flipping, until cooked through and deeply browned all over, 25 to 30 minutes.

Meanwhile, combine olives, garlic, parsley, the remaining 4 Tbsp. olive oil and 2 Tbsp. water in a small bowl; season with salt and pepper.

Once chicken is cooked, remove baking sheet from the oven and transfer chicken to a large serving platter, leaving behind any of the juices and bits stuck to the paper in the pan. Scrape all bits from the paper and leave in the pan.

Make sure the baking sheet is on a sturdy surface (the stovetop, a counter), then pour the olive mixture onto the sheet. Using a spatula or wooden spoon, gently scrape up all the bits of chicken left behind, letting the olive mixture mingle with the rendered fat and get increasingly saucy. Pour olive mixture over the chicken, then serve.

INGREDIENTS:

- 3 ½ lb. bone-in, skin-on chicken parts, legs and thighs please
- 1 tsp. ground turmeric
- 6 Tbsp. olive oil, separated (meaning in two different amounts, here and there)
- Kosher salt and ground pepper
- ½ c. white wine vinegar or champagne vinegar
- 1 ½ c. green Castelvetrano olives, crushed and pitted, buy the best
- 2 garlic cloves, finely grated or pressed
- 1 c. fresh parsley leaves, chopped

Pair with 2021 Dresser Winery Lajur

Pickled Onions

Pickled anything involves vinegar.

DIRECTIONS:

In a small, non-reactive saucepan, heat the vinegar, sugar, salt, seasonings and chile until boiling.

Add the onion slices and lower heat, then simmer gently for 30 seconds.

Remove from heat and let cool completely.

Transfer the onions and the liquid into a jar then refrigerate until ready to use.

Storage: The onions will keep for several months, but I find they're best the week they're made.

INGREDIENTS:

- 3/4 c. (180ml) white vinegar
- 3 Tbsp. (50g) sugar
- pinch of salt
- 1 bay leaf
- 5 allspice berries
- 5 whole cloves
- A small, dried chili pepper
- 1 large red onion, peeled and thinly sliced into rings

From my friend Liz Wilkes.

Grain Salad

DIRECTIONS:

Bring a pot of salted water to a boil. Add barley and cook according to directions on the package.

Drain and place in a large bowl. Cool.

Make the dressing.

Toast the spices in a dry skillet over medium heat, tossing, until fragrant, about 3 minutes.

Remove from heat and finely chop or use a spice grinder.

Put in a small bowl and whisk in vinegar and mustard. Slowly whisk in the EVOO and season to taste.

Add chickpeas, feta, dill, arugula and lemon juice to the barley and toss, then add the vinaigrette and toss to coat. Serve cold.

No idea where I found this recipe.

INGREDIENTS:

Vinaigrette:

- 1 tsp. coriander seeds
- 1 tsp. cumin seeds
- 1 tsp. fennel seeds
- 1/4 c. olive oil
- 2 Tbsp. white wine vinegar
- 1 tsp. Dijon mustard
- Salt and pepper

Salad:

- 1 c. barley
- 1 can chickpeas, rinsed (15 oz), or your own home cooked beans
- 4 ounces feta, crumbled
- 3 Tbsp. chopped fresh dill
- 5 oz. arugula
- 2 Tbsp. lemon juice

Pair with 2022 Dresser Winery Sigh-La Rosé

You see the last ingredient, lemon juice. I did not write *L is for lemon* and for that I am surprised. Because there are literally 100 things you can do with a Meyer lemon. Check it out.

But I digress.

The newspaper section is a wonderful place to find great recipes. When I lived in the Bay Area, I read the Chronicle. When we moved to the Central Coast, I did what my grandmother did. I read the *L.A. Times*. Great recipes. Then I found the *NYTimes*. OMG. Love their food section too. It may be the best. That list for lemons is a perfect example of the great things you can find in the newspaper. Support the newspapers. At this point in our history, it is one of the only safeguards left for the truth to be told. Yes, it may be biased, but it has real news in it. And, if they get it wrong, there are actual corrections issued.

You can use vinegar to clean things. *Reader's Digest* published a list. Here is the link.

And, did I mention I love vinegar? It is a miracle food and cleaner. So cool.

W is for Watermelon

Watermelon is a seasonal fruit like just about every other fruit on the planet. I recommend that if watermelon is a main ingredient in a recipe, don't use-out of season watermelon. Just don't. Wait until it is hot and watermelons are local and in supply.

Having said that, there are so many ways to carve a watermelon and kids and adults alike, love a carved watermelon. So give it a try. There is a website , watermelon.org with lots of great ideas. Be the life of the party and bring your watermelon to a summer party. People will talk about it forever. It is just that good.

Here is a recipe that you can use in carved watermelon.

Watermelon & Tomato Salad

DIRECTIONS:

Whisk $1/4$ cup champagne vinegar or white wine vinegar, 3 tsp. sugar, 2 tsp. kosher salt and $1/4$ tsp. cayenne together in a small bowl. Quarter and thinly slice half a small red onion and toss it in the vinegar mixture. Set aside to let rest until the onion softens and mellows, about 30 minutes.

Remove the rind from a 4-lb. piece of seedless watermelon, cut into 1" chunks, and transfer to a large bowl. Cut stemmed and cored ripe tomatoes into 1" chunks. Combine the tomatoes with the watermelon.

Pour in the onion-vinegar mixture along with $1/4$ cup extra-virgin olive oil and toss gently with your hands. Add 1 cup each loosely packed basil and mint and toss gently. Season with kosher salt and freshly ground pepper, to taste.

Serve salad at room temperature on its own or alongside grilled fish or meat. Serves quite a few. If you use a bigger melon, size ingredients appropriately.

And that, my dear reader, is my only watermelon recipe. It is that good.

INGREDIENTS:

- $1/4$ c. champagne vinegar
- 3 tsp. sugar
- 1 tsp. kosher salt
- $1/4$ tsp. cayenne - or to taste
- $1/2$ small red onion, quartered and thinly sliced
- 4 lb. watermelon, rind removed and cut into 1" chunks - seedless is easier
- $1 1/2$ lb. tomatoes cored and ripe - or use cherry tomatoes sliced in half lengthwise
- $1/4$ c. extra virgin olive oil
- 1 c. basil, loosely packed, roughly torn
- 1 c. mint, loosely packed, roughly torn
- salt and pepper

Here is a website that presents several carving ideas:

Of course, if you want to carve the rind, buy a second melon. I have used a melon baller to remove the fruit from the rind. That works too.

Adapted from *Saveur* magazine issue #113.

X is for Xmas Cookies

Before I share two recipes, let me recommend that you always have parchment paper on hand in your kitchen. For cookies, for one-pan meals. Rayman loves me and parchment. Makes clean up much easier. Also good for transferring hot, just-out-of-the-oven cookies to a cooling rack. And you do have a few cooling racks, don't you?

No holiday is complete, if you are a cook, without cookies.

This is a given. And over the years, I have collected some great recipes. Here are two of my favorites.

Mexican Tea Cakes are to die for. They may be called other names, but this is the name I use. Call them what you want. It is our absolute favorite cookie. And it is relatively easy.

Mexican Tea Cakes

DIRECTIONS:

Beat together butter and 1/2 cup confectioners sugar in a large bowl with an electric mixer at moderately high speed until pale and fluffy, about 4 minutes. Beat in vanilla, then add flour, pecans, and salt and mix at low speed until just combined. Chill, wrapped in wax paper at least 6 hours.

Preheat oven to 375°F.

Let dough stand at room temperature until just pliable, about 15 minutes. Roll level teaspoons of dough into
3/4-inch balls and arrange about 2 inches apart on lightly buttered large baking sheets.

Sift remaining 2 1/2 cups confectioners sugar into a large shallow

INGREDIENTS:

- 2 sticks (1 cup) unsalted butter, softened
- 3 c. confectioners sugar
- 1 tsp. vanilla
- 2 1/4 c. all-purpose flour
- 3/4 c. very finely chopped pecans (2 1/2 oz)
- 3/4 tsp. salt

bowl.

Bake in batches in middle of oven until bottoms are pale golden, 8 to 10 minutes. Immediately transfer hot cookies to confectioners sugar, gently rolling to coat well, then transfer to a rack to cool completely. Some will crumble — eat them!

Roll cookies in confectioners sugar again

Spoon Cookies

These are another hit of a cookie, similar but quite different than Mexican Tea Cakes.

DIRECTIONS:

Make dough:

Note: Dough can be made 12 hours before baking and chilled, covered. Bring to room temperature to soften slightly before forming cookies, about 30 minutes.

Fill kitchen sink or large, deep pan with about 2 inches of cold water. Melt butter in a 2- to 3-quart heavy saucepan over moderate heat and cook, stirring occasionally, until butter turns golden and the butter develops a nut like fragrance, and flecks on bottom of pan turn a rich caramel brown, 10 to 12 minutes. (Butter will initially foam, then dissipate. A thicker foam will appear and cover the surface just before butter begins to brown; stir more frequently toward end of cooking.) Place pan in sink or large pan holding the water to stop the cooking, then cool, stirring frequently, until butter starts to look opaque, about 4 minutes. Remove the sauce pan from sink and stir in sugar and vanilla. If you burn the butter, throw it out and start anew.

Whisk together flour, baking soda, and salt in a small bowl and stir into butter mixture until a dough forms. Shape into a ball, wrap with plastic wrap, and let stand at cool room temperature 1 to 2 hours (to allow flavors to develop).

INGREDIENTS:

- 2 sticks (1 cup) cold unsalted butter, cut into pieces
- 3/4 c. sugar
- 2 tsp. vanilla
- 2 c. all-purpose flour
- 1 tsp. baking soda
- 1/8 tsp. salt, slightly rounded
- 1/3 c. fruit preserves (your choice)

SPECIAL EQUIPMENT

- A deep-bowled teaspoon (not a measuring spoon)

The recipe gets it name from the use of the spoon to shape the cookies.

Form and bake cookies:

Put oven rack in middle position and preheat oven to 325°F.

Press a piece of dough into bowl of teaspoon, flattening top, then slide out and place, flat side down, on an ungreased baking sheet. (Dough will feel crumbly, but will become cohesive when pressed.) I use parchment paper. Continue forming cookies and arranging on sheet. Bake cookies until just pale golden, 8 to 15 minutes. Cool cookies on sheet on a rack 5 minutes, then transfer cookies to rack and cool completely, about 30 minutes.

Assemble cookies:

While cookies cool, heat preserves in a small saucepan over low heat until just runny, then pour through a sieve into a small bowl, pressing hard on solids, and cool completely.

Spread the flat side of a cookie with a thin layer of preserves. Sandwich with flat side of another cookie. Continue with remaining cookies and preserves, then let stand until set, about 45 minutes. Transfer cookies to an airtight container and wait 2 days before eating. Good luck with this part. They are hard to leave alone.

You will love these cookies, too.

Feel free to make these X-mas cookies year around. Why not? Unnecessary rules are unnecessary.

There are hundreds of cookie recipes. This book is nearing completion. So, I'll leave it to the reader to discover their favorites on their own.

Y is for Yeasts

There is a fungus among us, and it is called yeast. A one-cell beast called yeast is something which we could not live without. Through the process of fermentation, yeast converts sugars into carbon dioxide and alcohol. These two byproducts make yeast an extremely useful tool in food production. And that is an understatement.

Wine and beer rely on fungus. Fungi are good and have been around since the dawn of civilization.

And, get this, Interesting Yeast Facts: A single cell of yeast is 3 to 5 microns in diameter. Visible colonies of yeast are composed of at least one million cells. A package of yeast used for cooking contains billions of cells. Good thing we don't buy yeast by the cell!!

So, without further ado, let me share with you a recipe that is a winner. Keep in mind, I mostly buy my bread and such at a couple of great bakeries we have locally, and I encourage you all to do the same. Boulangerie for the bread, baby!!

Let me also mention that there are bread machines. If you are busy and need or want homemade bread all the time, consider a machine. We had one. The reason we don't have one anymore is because we don't eat bread all the time. The machine takes up room. And, I like to support our local bakers.

Whole Wheat Bread

A word about this recipe. It is famous. It is easy. It is tasty.

DIRECTIONS:

In a medium bowl, stir together the flours, salt, and yeast. Add the water and blend into the mix with a wooden spoon or your hand until you have a sticky dough. Cover the bowl and let sit at room temperature for 12 to 18 hours. You should see the dough double in size and become pock-marked with bubbles.

When the first rise is done, scrap it out of the bowl in one piece onto a lightly floured surface, using your flour-dusted hands or a scrapper. Nudge it into a round ball, first lifting the edges toward the middle. Then tuck the edges of the dough to make it round,

Place a tea towel on your work space and generously dust it with cornmeal or flour. Gently place the dough on the tea towel, seam side down. Fold the tea towel over the dough to cover it and then put it in a draft free place or warming oven on proof setting for 1 or 2 hours. The dough will almost double in size, and when you touch it, your finger print should hold the impression. If it springs back, allow it to rise 15 minutes or so. Then test again.

$1/2$ hour before the second rise ends, move the oven rack to the lower third of the oven. Preheat the oven to 475F and immediately place your pot in the oven. I use cast iron and recommend that you do the same. (4 $1/2$ to 5 12 quart with lid will suffice.)

INGREDIENTS:

- 2 $1/4$ c. bread flour
- $3/4$ c. whole wheat flour
- Salt
- $1/2$ tsp. Yeast. I use active dry yeast or instant dry yeast
- Cool water (55 to 65F)
- Cornmeal for dusting

Using pot holders, carefully remove the preheated pot from the oven and uncover. Quickly unfold the tea towel and invert the dough into the pot, seam side up. Cover the pot, return it to the oven, and bake for 30 minutes.

Open the oven, remove the lid and continue baking until the bread is a deep chestnut color, about 15-30 minutes more. Then remove from the oven wearing good mitts, and place on a rack to cool thoroughly.

I have discovered that it is hard to throw that bread into the pot. You might try letting it rise on a piece of parchment and then lowering the dough into the pot by using the parchment like a sling. Or tin foil. Just a thought.

Creamed Biscuits

DIRECTIONS:

Heat the oven to 425°F or less if using convection.

Combine the flour, salt, baking powder and sugar in a mixing bowl, stirring with a fork to blend.

Slowly add the cream to the dry ingredients, stirring, until the dough holds together. Knead gently on a lightly-floured surface for about 1 minute. Pat the dough into a 1/2-inch thick circle and use a sharp knife to cut it into 8 biscuits. Or you could use a biscuit cutter.

Arrange the wedges 2 inches apart on an ungreased baking sheet and brush the tops of the biscuits with melted butter. I like to dip the biscuits into the butter for the luxury of it. Bake for 12-15 minutes, until lightly browned. Serve warm with plenty of butter and/or honey, or jam.

There was no yeast in this recipe. However, it is such a good bake, I felt compelled to include it. It is adapted from Marion Cunningham.

INGREDIENTS:

- 2 c. all purpose flour
- 1 tsp. kosher salt
- 1 Tbsp. baking powder
- 1 tsp. sugar
- 1 to 1 1/2 c. heavy cream, poured in judicially
- Melted butter

 is for Zebra

Oh, I suppose Z could also have been titled "Z is for Zabaglione" but I don't have any stories about zabaglione. Zebras, yes. Zabaglione, no.

So this morning we were out in the 'hood' walking the dog when I was relaying my story of how I woke up around 2 a.m. and when I couldn't go back to sleep, I decided to decide that "Z" would be the next topic for my book. I then said to the Rayman that since there weren't many words that began with a Z that I had settled for zebra. Then the Rayman, who is fluent in cooking, but not overly so, piped up and said, "There's zucchini." Oh, for heaven's sake. How could I forget zucchini, the ubiquitous green tube of a vegetable? You know the one that people plant too many of, say two, and then have zucchini coming out of their ears? Yes, that zucchini. It had escaped me! So, in light of the fact that I did not show the proper amount of respect for this grows-like-a-weed veggie, I will share with you my favorite zucchini recipe which is adapted from Marcella Hazan's *Classic Italian Cook Book*. It is fried zucchini and it is addictive, so much so that I rarely make it, what with all the clamoring about obesity.

Here it is, and it serves four to six.

Deep fried Zucchini

DIRECTIONS:

Clean the zucchini and cut them lengthwise into ⅛-inch slices. I like to cut the zucchini in half lengthwise and lay it down on the cutting board and then it cut it in half and then make my zucchini "sticks."

Put a cup of water in a pie plate and gradually add flour, sifting it through a strainer and beating it constantly with a fork until the all the flour is added. It should resemble sour cream in consistency.

Heat the oil over high. When the oil is very hot, dip the zucchini in the batter and then slip only enough in the oil so that they fit loosely. Too many will cause the oil to lose heat and that is a bad thing. You will end up with soggy zucchini.

When a golden crust has formed on the bottom side, turn them over. When both sides have a nice crust, remove the zucchini and place them on paper towels to drain. Sprinkle with salt. When you've done all the zucchini, serve immediately. And don't be like me and leave the stove on. It will not end well.

This is so easy that unless you burn yourself on the oil, drop the zucchini on the floor, or find out you don't have enough flour etc. you'll go to this classic again and again.

Also, only make this if you are serving something else with it that requires little labor at the end, like a roast, or a steak. Actually those are perfect suggestions because cooked meat must rest. Most people don't understand the concept of meat resting. That, or they are always so hungry to eat that they say the hell with it and cut right into the meat when it is hot off the grill. This will not make for a juicy piece of meat. The meat juices will run right out and you will be disappointed. Let your meat rest.. .at least 15 minutes, and better yet, 20 minutes. This will give you time to fry that zucchini and toss that salad.

Really. I am serious. Let it rest. Set the timer and stick to the game plan.

Oh, one more addition on the zucchini. This one is for Tamara, the great zucchini grower in our lives!!

INGREDIENTS:

- 1 lb. of zucchini
- ⅔ c. of all-purpose flour
- Vegetable oil that fills the fry pan ¾ inches
- Salt

Zucchini Chowder

DIRECTIONS:

Heat a stovetop pressure cooker over medium heat or set an electric cooker to sauté. Add the onion and dry sauté for 1 minute. Add the garlic and sauté another minute. Add the squash, lentils, almond flour, and stock.

Lock on the lid. Bring the cooker to high pressure. Cook for 4 minutes. Let the pressure come down naturally for at least 10 minutes. Remove the lid, carefully tilting it away from you.

Stir in the nutritional yeast. Using an immersion blender, blender, or food processor, blend soup until creamy.

Add salt and pepper to taste. Pour into bowls and serve, garnished with basil.

INGREDIENTS:

- 2 c. finely chopped onion
- 3 cloves garlic, minced
- 4 c. zucchini or summer squash of any kind, cut into 2-inch chunks. (I recommend avoiding bigger zucchinis.)
- ¼ c. ground red lentils
- ¼ c. almond flour or meal
- 2 c. vegetable stock
- ¼ c. nutritional yeast
- Salt and freshly ground black pepper
- ¼ c. minced fresh basil, for garnish

Now with zucchini out of the way, where was I? Oh, yes. Zebras.

As indicated earlier in this tome, there was a trip to Africa. And that is where I saw a zebra killed by a lion and then eaten by lions...at least at the beginning of the feast. Many people to whom I have relayed this story, have mentioned that they would not be able to watch. Too gruesome. Too bloody, etc. Their point is taken but I didn't find it that way at all. The kill was quick. Over in a few a seconds really. Poor zebra was grazing and apparently didn't pick up the scent of the lions... to its detriment.

Secondly, this is life. Eat or be eaten. When I walked from the restaurant to my room, an armed guard was required although I'm not sure what good that would do. Those lions were quick.

The other thing about zebras is that there are a lot of them in Kenya and Tanzania. While only 1/5 of the chimpanzees still survive from their earlier numbers, zebras and wildebeest abound. It is breathtaking to see them in large numbers. Not like any zoo you would ever go to. So, the point of this point is to say that zebra is served in restaurants.

The last night of our trip we ended up in Nairobi and as a tour group were taken to a restaurant named Carnivore. It was great theatre. As I recall it was a building with a high ceiling in the shape of a cone, perhaps thatched. There was a huge pit of burning logs in the center of the room. That is where the cooking of the zebra took place. They cooked other pieces of meat as well. Beef comes to mind. Pork. Regular stuff along with exotic cuts.

We were steered to our table where servers brought pieces of meat on trays or skewers, and then asked what we would like. I chose beef, I think. No zebra here. Too adventuresome for me. But really? Zebra? They look so much like a horse, and I have no experience eating horse. Some receptor in my brain just went cuckoo and wouldn't allow me to order zebra. Nothing cerebral going on there. Of course, I now regret not eating zebra. It would make such an interesting story.

Here is a good link if you want to know about zebras and hear them bray.

In reading about zebras, I discovered that lions are color blind. Who knew?

But, I digress. And like all good things, this book must end, and ending it in Africa is as good as place as any. Africa is the trip that tops all my trips. It is indescribable. Life and death on display.

I remember the first night in Tanzania. We were driving after dark to reach the Ngorongoro Crater when there he was. A grand male lion sauntering down the road we were on. The silly woman to my left rolled down the window of the Range Rover we were in. At which point I shrieked, "Shut the window." Did it not occur to her that the lion could attack? Well, it may not have occurred to her, but it certainly did to me. Apparently I suffer from a strong desire to live. But to see that magnificent animal in the headlights of the Rover was breathtaking. So self assured. So big. So, well, beastly.

That was when we found out that the lodges in Tanzania turn off the generators at night, at which time Africa becomes truly the deepest, darkest place. The other thing was that the water system went on the blink that night so we couldn't shower or flush the toilets...not good. About 3 a.m. I heard water running so I jumped up and took a shower. A very cold one. Oh, my.

We toured the crater the next day and saw lots of animals. At one point we came across a pride of lions (females). The guide turned the motor off and we sat and watched. The lions were perched on some boulders. Since it was hot, our vehicle interested them because it threw off shade. So three of them came to the Rover and laid down in the shade. Too exciting. We were all atwitter.

Every day brought new adventures inside that Rover. The way the trips were conducted in Africa, there were two game rides a day. Early morning and late afternoon because this is the time of the day when the animals are most active. The most unpleasant time in that Rover was when we made a mad dash across the landscape to arrive at the Olduvai Gorge...a big hole in the ground where old human remains were found. The mad dash consisted of eating pounds of dust. We all looked like the Old West Bandidos as portrayed by Hollywood in the western movies. We had bandanas and scarves tied around our heads in an effort to keep the dust out of our mouths. The dust was being kicked up by the Rover because we were not traveling on Interstate 10...but on a road that was a glorified rut.

Along with the pounds of dust, our innards got involuntarily rearranged from all the jostling we suffered as we lurched from one side of the "road" to the other trying to avoid "potholes". Suffice it to say, avoid the O. Gorge. It's not worth it, in my opinion.

The day after we arrived in Nairobi, the capitol of Kenya, we found ourselves back at the Nairobi airport for a flight in a very small, low flying prop plane to Arusha, Tanzania. Tanzania was where the famed Serengeti was located. It is still located there.

Upon arriving at this dusty, ill-equipped airport, my stomach was not happy as the small plane got thrown all over the sky by the updrafts welling up from the desert-like land below us. This was a busy airport so I was more than horrified by the condition of the restrooms in the passenger area. The toilets didn't flush, and it appeared to me that they had never flushed. It shocked my sensibilities but this was just one of many places that made relieving myself a major problem in Africa.

After that experience it was then time to face the Customs people in the "terminal". When it was my turn to have my paper documents inspected, the agent told me in a very thick British accent, that I did not have my proof of vaccination for yellow fever, and thus I could not enter the country. So, consider this. I had just flown for almost 2 days to join a tour that this guy was telling me I could not join because I didn't have proper documentation. Further, he said, "You must get a shot and spend 10 days in Tanzania, before you can take your tour, Madam."

In retrospect, I was a member of Kaiser and they administered all required shots, I was told. So with that assurance, I jumped in head first and told the man, "There is no way I can get a shot here (it was at the height of AIDS), and I cannot wait 10 days until I can join the tour, because the tour will be over." The man did not seem to be bothered by my pushback. My uncle in the meantime was horror struck at the idea that I could not carry on so he whispered to me that I should bribe him. "With what exactly,?" I sputtered. "Money. Try money."

Given the situation, I grew bold, and apologized for this incident to the man-in-charge. "Perhaps $20 American cash could help resolve this issue?", I bravely proceeded. The man, let's call him Shorty, seemed interested. He scratched his chin, looked away, and restarted the conversation by saying, "I was admiring that animal skinned fountain pen hanging around your neck." Slyly I signaled agreement by taking the pen off and presenting it to him and then I fished out of my teeny-weanie money holder, an Andrew Jackson bill and thrust it forward in my closed hand. He took both items and stamped my paperwork. Mission accomplished. I was free to wander about Tanzania with fear and foreboding in my heart. Would I get bitten by a mosquito and get yellow fever and suffer organ failure? Did I really not have the shot? It was a mystery to me. And it was a complete upset to my uncle, who to hear him tell it, had never, ever made a mistake when traveling.

Henceforth, the entire time I was in Africa, my biggest fear was mosquitos…not lions or hyenas (that had just eaten a person whose car had broken down)….but mosquitos since they were the carriers of yellow fever. I wore Deet everywhere. Lots of Deet. Deet and I became best friends. Never mind that it can't be good for you, all those chemicals. Yellow fever was probably worse. So, I was for the rest of the trip, the Deet queen of Africa.

The lodges in Tanzania were wonderful. Modern. Interesting architecturally speaking. On the Serengeti, this was terrific because you are out in the middle of nowhere. Like the lodge at the Ngorongoro Crater, the water in the bathrooms were cold and they turned off the generators at night. This was a problem for seeing things in the dark.

One night after lights out, I heard strange noises in the room. What on earth was that, I wondered. What type of animal or insect had invaded my room. I laid in the bed in abject fear…listening. The noise continued. Do army ants make noise? I ruled out snakes, they slither oh, so silently. What was it? I called out to my Uncle Ralph who was in the next room informing him that I couldn't find my flashlight. He said he'd meet me at the door with his flashlight which he did.

After closing the door, I turned on the flashlight and shined it on the window in my room, and then I let out a blood curdling scream. What I saw was an image of ME, but so afraid was I by this time, that my reaction was instantaneous (and very loud) and came out before my head had time to process the information. It was ME. With that, I gave up the search, returned to my bed, hid under the cover and lay listening to the roar of lions which started about 15 minutes later. It was priceless.

In those days, circa 1988, the digital camera had not come along, and so what I was left with was a camera, which had a telephoto lens about the size of a baseball bat and the weight of a 5 pound-dumbbell, which I wore around my neck. Then there was the movie camera that was ensconced in a suitcase, and it weighed about 20 pounds... and the camera itself was about as big as an Amazon box full of a 6-month supply of cereal. I carried the movie camera in the provided suitcase. So, I was completely outfitted but very, very uncomfortable. But, alas, it was Africa and I had to record our trip with all manners of cameras. Did I mention that Uncle Ralph was not interested in taking pictures? So, it was incumbent on me to "catch" our trip on film...which I dutifully did, and now I have albums of pictures I rarely look at and a movie that almost caused a family squabble because Rayman had seen the video one too many times.

Actually in his defense, once was probably enough. It was unedited and completely boring in parts. And the technology of the time was the VCR. I don't know if we even have a machine that will play the darn thing. Times they are a'changing. So I haven't seen the movie, literally, in years. But I have it and I always will until I'm dead and gone and my survivors will find it and not be able to play it and they will throw it in the garbage. Or they might find a way to play it and then throw it in the garbage. Oh, well.

This is Uncle Ralph with some Masai boys.

But I digress. There are a few treasured pictures of elephants, lions, me and the Masai children which I have scattered around the house. They always make me smile. There are stories there, you know.

Editor's Note: There are no recipes for zebra so don't look for any. It was not an oversight. As Anne Byrn of substack fame says, "We're done here."

Finis.

Index of Recipes

IN ALPHABETICAL ORDER

Achiote Chicken	44
Adult Pimiento Cheese	52
Albacore Grilled with Mint Sauce	55
Angel Pie	85
Artichokes on the barbie	11
Banana sandwich	15
Beans in the Pot	17
Black Bottom Pie	23
Bread	131
Brussels to Love	51
Cacio and Pepe	97
Chicken with Vinegar and Olives	120
Creamed Biscuits	132
Dates Stuffed with Goat Cheese and Almonds	28
Deep Fried Zucchini	134
Duck Legs	71
Focaccia	48
Frozen Praline & Banana Parfait	32
Gateau Mousse a la Nectarine	87
Grain Salad	122
Jambalaya	105
Macarons	82
Mexican Tea Cakes	127
Molten Chocolate Cake	25
Mousse au Chocolat	35

Nectarine Blueberry Crisp 90
Onion Panade 93
Pesto 57
Pickled Onions 121
Roast Chicken... 40
Roasted Cranberry Sauce 63
Roasted Red Potatoes with Garlic and Rosemary 50
Shakshouka... 112
Spaghetti with Green Garlic 53
Spoon Cookies 128
Watermelon & Tomato Salad 125
Zucchini Chowder... 135

Acknowledgements

As I am wont to do, I march to a different drummer at times.
This is one of those times.

Grandma Bird inspired me. Here she is modeling her graduation dress circa 1916.

Below her is a picture of the Rayman, my foil. He is the just the best at encouraging me to do what I have been doing, whether it be cooking, writing, golfing, paddling, you name it. He is my inspiration for fun-loving stories. He's here with son, Ryan.

Additionally, I am indebted to my "editors-in-chiefs" Nancy Cleland and Mary Kay Bornfleth.

This is Nancy in her kitchen. You haven't lived until you work with Nancy and Mary Kay to make sure every I is dotted, every T is crossed. Every comma in its place. So much fun.

A picture of Mary Kay and her husband, Jay. They are related to us through our doggies, Jaycee and Beau.

Tamara Greenwell has had a huge influence on me. With her bravery and her ambition, she sets the tone. A fabulous daugher-in-law. Simply the best. And she lured me into dragon boat racing. How about that? And son, Ryan, was my original mark. Wanting to write a cookbook for the kid morphed into a cookbook for the kids. They are grown adults now but I still call them kids. When we have vanished from this world, this tome will live on. Mission Accomplished!!

Becky Dresser, the artichoke artist. I appreciate her willingness to draw the artichoke. We are related, albeit, distantly.

Jo Ellen appears in some of the key stories in this book. She is quite a dish in her own right. She had a major influence on me and I so appreciate it.

Several friends helped me immensely by their success. Linda Connors Healy, a high school friend, published a book. Margaret Bertrand published a book. So did Eileen Shibley. So did Kathy Mastako. So did Ron Zell. Jerry Sheldon wrote a book and shared it. These remarkable people inspired me as did Colleen Craig. I'm blessed to be friends with these people. They are so cool. Thank you all.

A special shout-out to all the recipes I found because these amazing people were around to inspire. Julia Child, Suzanne Goin, Marian Cunningham, Judy Rodgers, Alice Waters, Gordon Ramsey, Jim Haley, Nancy Silverton, Marcella Hazan, The Two Hot Tamales, Diane Kennedy, John Ash, writers at Saveau, Gourmet, Fine Cooking, LA Times, NYTimes, Cook's Illustrated and all the others. My friends Liz Wilkes, Eileen Shibley, Larry Viselli, nephew Christopher Nelson, Greg and Teri Morrow, Neta Davis, Audrey Gendron, Karen Watts, Rita Rice, cousin Sue Jessie, Ruth and Tom Donnelly, K.C. and Jake Covert, Bob Dodge and Margaret Bertrand, Flo Bartel, Dorothy and Alan Buck, Janice and Terry Packer., Brandon Duff, Jeff Green, Shary and John Goulart, Sandy and Ted Olsen, Chris Oswald, Deb and Jack Grisanti, Colette Yamaguchi, Al DeVico and Charlie Aron, Mary Qualls and Jim Sundheim, Diane Wyatt, Connie Edwards, Donnie Bryan, Robin and Paul Slocum, Pat Smith, Tim and Bev Hardwick, Bob and Carol Kerwin, Marsha Boring, Seabrook Griffin, Anne R. Allen and the SLO Nightwriters group, Colleen Craig…and so many more. If I left you out, I am so sorry. An embarrassment of riches.

Ben Lawless, the man behind the design of this book who worked tirelessly on putting it together and getting it on to Amazon. Without him, this book would not have been published. Ben is located in Atascadero, CA. The name of his business is Penciled In.

*Dresser Winery and Luxury Vacation Rental Villa
5530 Dresser Ranch Pl, Paso Robles, CA 93446*

And last but not least, Kory and Catherine Burke, owners of the Dresser Winery that provided the wine paring. They graciously took the time and made the effort to do this for me. The backstory is that their winery is located on Dresser Ranch Place.

Turns out my family owned the Dresser ranch from 1882 until the mid-70s when my uncle, Ralph Dresser, started selling off parcels of the ranch. Only one lot remains in the family today. I love that they named the winery Dresser!!

And get this. Kory is a history buff. It was meant to be!! My next book entitled *From Beloit to Clark Gable in Three Generations* is a book about how the ranch came to be. I'm overhanging the market as the book is still being written.

And for the final picture of the book, our dear doggie, Beau. He keeps us walking, laughing, and sane!!

Made in the USA
Monee, IL
16 August 2023

40906129R00085